Overcoming the Fear of Death

ALSO BY *David Cole Gordon*

SELF-LOVE

Overcoming the Fear of Death

David Cole Gordon

The Macmillan Company

The Macmillan Company
866 Third Avenue, New York, N. Y. 10022
Collier-Macmillan Canada Ltd., Toronto, Ontario

Library of Congress Catalog Card Number: 73-126192

FIRST PRINTING

Printed in the United States of America

To my Mother—Tessie Cole Gordon

AND

My Children—Lesley Dara, Marc Seth, and Alicia Beth

AND

As Always—for Pearl

IN MEMORIAM

Amelia Metrani

This book is also dedicated to the memory of Amelia Metrani—a gifted pianist and teacher, and a warm friend—one of whose last acts was to read this book and suggest several important critical revisions.

Acknowledgment

THIS BOOK IS also for my editor-friends who have read it in manuscript and have made many wise and useful suggestions, most of which have been adopted in whole or in part. I am grateful for their friendship, generous assistance, and comprehension of my work: Robert Powell, Robert Walter Marks, Roy Fairfield, Alan Rinzler, Peter Matson, Robert Briggs, Felix Morrow, and "Cap" Pearce.

Contents

1 *The Fear of Death* 13

2 *Antidotes to the Fear of Death—Work, Money, and Synthetic Immortality* 25

3 *The Fear of Losing Time* 31

4 *The Fear of Decay, Irreversibility, and the Unknown* 41

5 *The Fear of Life—The Pain of Living* 49

6 *The Fear of the Loss of Self and the Cessation of Thought* 65

7 *The Fear of the Loss of Pleasure* 83

8 *Life and a Theory of Unification* 89

9 *Death and Unification* 101

10 *Conclusion* 111

Overcoming the Fear of Death

I

The Fear of Death

Our lives are poisoned by a fear of death, and much of our culture represents a response, however inadequate, to this fear. Most of us are afraid to contemplate our own ending; and when anything reminds us that we too shall die, we flee and turn our thoughts to happier matters. The thought of our finitude and ephemerality is so frightening that we run away from this basic fact of existence, consciously and unconsciously, and proceed through life as though we shall endure forever. When we recognize the inevitability of death by the making out of our wills and buying life insurance, it is as though the wills and the insurance related to someone other than ourselves, and we live our actual life as though death is not likely to touch *us.* Insofar as we consider the possibility of our own death at all, it is as an event that is as remote as the end of time, and so we tend unconsciously to repress the fear and the fact of our ultimate doom, or consciously to forget it.

Forgetting may be defined as: to lose remembrance of, or

to cease to retain in one's memory. Forgetting may be either a conscious or an unconscious mechanism and phenomenon. The classic delineation of unconscious forgetting is Freud's psychoanalytical theory of repression, which is the so-called foundation stone of the contemporary analytic understanding of neuroses. Freud defined repression operationally as: "The infantile ego, under the domination of the external world, disposes of undesirable instinctual demands by means of what are called repressions."* The essence of repression is in the function of rejecting and keeping something out of consciousness. But we are conscious of our finitude, are we not? We know that someday death will come to us too. Nevertheless, we are constantly engaged in consciously trying to forget it. We cannot repress it in a true psychoanalytical sense, since there are too many constant reminders of it. Death, however, is something that happens to others, and it is virtually impossible for us to comprehend our own eventual demise. Do we not really live with the notion that we are immortal, and push the inevitability of our decease far into the remotest recesses of consciousness?

Insofar as we live with a fundamental belief which is untrue, is not much of our life converted into a lie? Is it not true that we will die, and that this very moment may be our last? It is the fear of death which is responsible for our refusing even to face the facts of life and death. If we can eliminate the fear of death, then we can perhaps work a

* Sigmund Freud, *An Outline of Psychoanalysis,* trans. James Strachey, New York, W. W. Norton & Co., 1949, p. 118.

transformation of our life. A change would mean that we would live with the fact that we are finite. Might it not perhaps also work a powerful and revolutionary change in many of our human relationships, and in other aspects of our lives as well?

But the fear of death is not easily overcome. Many of our greatest philosophers and psychotherapists, like Sigmund Freud, have been frightened by the spectre of death. Their erudition has provided little consolation when they came up against this problem. Indeed, aside from the suffering which is part of the human condition itself, the conundrum of death has not only baffled many of the greatest minds, but has perhaps been the chief reason why men have turned to the study of theology, philosophy, psychology, and medicine. Schopenhauer expressed the opinion that death is the "muse of philosophy." But the anxiety over death is not exclusive to the great thinkers. It afflicts all to some degree, regardless of age, sex, or religion.

Those who do not live by the dream that they are immortal, nevertheless live by the illusion of actuarial tables, which they believe guarantee them a definite life span. This belief, or illusion, is just as great a dream. Barring suicide, man's life span is not within his control, and this exception can certainly be questioned from a psychoanalytical as well as a common sense viewpoint. It is, of course, self-evident that man can perhaps prolong his life by proper diet and medical attention, and perhaps shorten it by addiction to alcohol, tobacco, and narcotics. But he cannot extend his life forever or, in most cases, even much beyond three score and ten. But he so deeply desires to endure, and is so afraid of dying, that most of his thoughts are future-oriented and largely revolve around anticipation of things to come.

Living by the fiction of immortality creates many of our basic human problems and conflicts. If man can look forward to an indefinite life span, he will continually think and plan ahead rather than live in the moment. He will constantly anticipate problems and things that may never materialize. He will mortgage the reality of the now for the dream and fantasy of the future.

Those who live in the belief that they are immortal are frequently so busy planning for the future, or acquiring material possessions, that they do not have time to be with those who cannot contribute to their material and financial aspirations. The moment is simply a transition point to the future, a future which may never arrive. They live in a state of constant tension, conflict, and confusion. There is conflict between the demands of the present and the self-imposed inexorable claims of the future.

The question *Can man live without continually thinking about, and providing for, the future?* suggests that he cannot. The fact is that he has rarely tried it. There is, of course, nothing contradictory in projecting into the future or planning for eventualities and contingencies to come. Nor is it meant to suggest that man is ever done with such activities as reading and thinking. But when planning is necessary, it should be done and then, "done with." If man could live with full realization of the tenuousness of his existence, and the fact that life is beyond his control, he could perhaps be more spontaneous and natural and "eat when he was hungry" and "sleep when he was tired"; he could perhaps meet every situation and everyone fresh, every moment, and not contaminate his personal contacts and meetings with old ideas, memories, and associations.

If we lived with the realization that this very moment might be our last, we would find that many problems and conflicts would evanesce, and life would be simplified and become more satisfying. How important is the choice of a necktie or dress if each moment might be our last? How important is the choice of any particular food or drink? How important is any petty annoyance when our life might end at any moment? How important is an unrealized dream under these circumstances?

Those who have lived with the knowledge of their finitude, and who have sometimes achieved renown, have lived each moment as though it was their last. It has been characteristic of those who have become one with themselves, their work, and the world. Great spiritual leaders have been marked by simplicity in dress, appearance, and manner. They do not exhaust their vital energy in the process of resolving conflicts over meaningless minutiae. Those who consciously realize that each moment may be their last, or who unconsciously live that way, generally do not hate, live for revenge, scheme, or seek material advantage. Familiar examples of such men are Socrates, Diogenes, Thoreau, Gandhi, Franklin Delano Roosevelt, and John F. Kennedy.

It might seem that living with the fact that every breath might be our last would tend to make man unhappy or depressed. The removal of the self-deceit which now overlays man's entire existence would perhaps relieve his chronic anxiety rather than feed it. Most men are not happy, but do not know why, and generally assign the causes to material reasons. They feel something is unnatural, but cannot quite figure out what it is. One of the key contradictions in life is that man lives in opposition to the way things really are, creating confusion and conflict. Removing his self-deceit by living life as it actually is, with full knowledge of his ephemerality and vulnerability, might enable man to relax and be more spontaneous. He could silence that small nagging voice within him that is subliminally and constantly reminding him that he is mortal. If he accepted his finitude, what he did then would perhaps become a new kind of doing. It would be a complete and concentrated doing, and man might be one with himself—and not doing one thing while thinking of another. If he lived each moment as though it would be his last, he could hopefully become one with the moment, the person he was with, the situation he was confronting, the world, and most importantly, one with himself.

Many men have been characterized by an intense fear of death during the early part of their lives, a fear which they have had to overcome on the way to achievement and greatness. Ernest Jones, Freud's biographer, relates Freud's fear of death: "Now, in Freud's personality there were several features of note in his attitude toward the topic of death. In the world of reality he was an unusually courageous man who faced misfortune, suffering danger and ultimately death itself with unflinching fortitude. But in phantasy there were other elements. As far back as we know anything of his life he seems to have been prepossessed by thoughts about death, more so than any other great man I can think of except perhaps Sir Thomas Browne and Montaigne. Even in the early years of our acquaintance he had the disconcerting habit of parting with the words, 'Goodbye; you may never see me again.' "* Freud suffered from repeated attacks of what he called *Todesangst* ("dread of death"). He hated the thought of growing old and once said he thought of death every day of his life. Jones felt that Freud had a curious longing for death and quotes a remark made by Freud after recovering from a fainting attack in Munich in 1912: "How sweet it must be to die." On the one hand, Freud feared that he might live as long as his half-brother or his father; on the other hand, he feared that he might die before his mother. He felt that his death would be terribly painful to her. While, quite obviously, concern for the effect of his death on his mother is not the same thing as a personal fear of death itself, both were aspects of Freud's *Todesangst.* Freud's attitude toward death was both rich and complicated, and he ascribed it to the effect of his death wishes in infancy.

A corollary of the *Todesangst* of "great men" has been their intense appreciation of life. The knowledge that life is ephemeral has been a spur to their work and their human-

* Ernest Jones, *The Life and Work of Sigmund Freud,* New York, Basic Books, 1957, Vol. 3, p. 279.

ity. It is suggested that no one who has not lost his fear of death can achieve true greatness.

Living with the constant fear of death, rather than just the awareness of death, contaminates life and adversely affects man's capacity to enjoy it. It is difficult, if not impossible, to live spontaneously and positively with joy if we are constantly fearful of losing all we have and are haunted with a sense of futility about all existence. Nor are these dark feelings attenuated by any of the religious teachings; they are, rather, enhanced by them, for the Christian religion, in particular, is premised upon the view that it is the life hereafter that really counts: this earthly life is important only insofar as it is a gateway. The Christian teachers never tire of pointing out that life is but an instant compared to the eternal after-life. Man is constantly enjoined to be on his guard and to avoid jeopardizing an eternal life of bliss for a passing moment of satisfaction, on what is, after all, only a way station en route to eternity.

Fear, in any form, is essentially a thought. If we can eliminate the thought *I fear death*, then we can perhaps dissipate the fear of death itself. But the fear of death is complex: it is a compound cluster of many psychological anxieties and fears rather than any single thought; these anxieties and fears may be collectively referred to as the fear of death. The composite comprising the fear of death includes the fear of time, the fear of decay, the fear of irreversibility, the fear of losing our pleasures and sensations, the fear of losing our thoughts and ability to think, and the fear of losing the self.

The desire to live is present from birth and perhaps exists even *in utero*. Any animal will struggle to live, to breathe, and to resist extinction. Physical survival is a primal instinctual phenomenon. It is of a different mode than the fear of death, which is a learned, conditioned, and acquired response. Insofar as we can know the mentality of other animals, it is not conceivable that they fear the possibility of death.

Casual observation and common sense tell us that clocks do not run backwards, physical and mental decay is irreversible, the unknown is to be feared, life is physical sensation and mental activity, and death is terminal. Of course, clocks can be made to run backwards, mechanically; and modern science posits a time reversal—possible in worlds of antimatter. And "casual observation" and "common sense" are peripheral in many ways to scientific and abstract thinking. But all of our thinking about life is based on the notion that it has a beginning which is birth, a middle which is the life we live, and an end which is death. Again, from a strictly scientific standpoint, one can say that "life" does not begin with birth, since there is a continuity of the germ plasm.

Virtually no thought has been given in the West to the period before man is born, and we treat it as though it did not exist. The Judeo-Christian religious tradition does not conceive of an existence prior to birth, other than the normal intrauterine fetal period. Certain Eastern religions do posit, however, reincarnation and successive rebirths; there are Yoga and Indian adepts who claim to be able to trace their previous incarnations. To most men, however, it is as though the world began with their earliest memories and recollections.

To many, the inquiry *Who was I before my birth?* might seem ridiculous, but it is one of the key *koans* employed by Zen masters in their efforts to awaken their disciples to the enlightenment and *satori* experience. However, the major concern of religion in the West has been, not with life before birth, but with life after death and allaying man's anxiety over his finitude. Much of the attraction that Western religion holds for man is based on the notion that it purports to know some answers to the nagging question of what happens to us after we die. It also offers the consolation of a continued life in some form, even though it may be one of eternal anguish, damnation, and torture.

It is just as logical and germane to ask *Who were we before our birth?* as it is to inquire *What happens to us after we die?* Both questions are important and useful if they lead to the inquiry *Who am I?* but they are futile and meaningless if the point of the queries is to determine whether we existed before birth, and will live after death, in the form with which we are most familiar, the skin-encapsulated entity we call *self*. While man has rarely examined the effect of the fear of death, it has had an all-pervasive influence on his life and culture.

As we stated in the opening paragraph of this chapter, much of our culture is primarily a response to man's fear of death. The culture which is then derived has, in turn, a causal effect which nurtures the fear of death. The following paradigm illustrates this oscillating, reciprocal bipolarity:

FEAR OF DEATH (*Cause*) ⇄ CULTURE (*Effect*)

Everything man does, builds, or creates, is in large measure designed to assuage his conscious or unconscious fear of oblivion, and the anguish of the realization that his life and death may be meaningless. So he attempts to succeed, make money, build monuments, do good work, have children, and prolong his physical existence as long as possible. He does all of this, knowing full well that he must die, and consciously represses, or forgets, his finitude and mortality.

Many of his endeavors are based on the desire to perpetuate his name and to make posterity aware of it. He erects a false or pseudo self by the process of egotistic affirmation. The nature of this self shall be discussed subsequently, in some detail. He evolves an elaborate structure of pride which serves as a bulwark against any assaults that are made on his hollow self. In his desire to persist he attempts to construct monuments on the largest possible scale and of the most enduring materials. From the flimsiest wooden cross to the pyramids of the Pharaohs of Egypt, man wishes to leave some reminder to people, as yet unborn, that he has lived.

Man's desire for immortal fame and glory is responsible for many of his literary, artistic, and other achievements. The desire for fame was one of the mainsprings of Freud's activity. The motivation behind the drive to build monolithic structures, create masterpieces, develop great systems, and do other great things, is the same desire to perpetuate the chimerical, egotistical affirmation of the false self that man primarily identifies with. Insofar as culture is defined in terms of material traits and artifacts, much of what man does and builds is motivated by his desire to endure. Can there be any question that it is also the mainspring of much of his other conduct and activity? Let us now examine the various antidotes man employs to assuage his fear of death, including work, money, and what we shall call synthetic immortality.

2

Antidotes to the Fear of Death— Work, Money, and Synthetic Immortality

WE SHALL ENDEAVOR in this chapter to show that the fear of death is so great and all pervasive, particularly when man grows older and the shadows lengthen and the shades get darker, that he consciously and unconsciously works to achieve synthetic immortality. His objective is frequently unconscious, and he is not aware that much of his activity basically represents a desire to perpetuate himself in some form. His true motivation is shrouded and veiled.

The desire to have children frequently represents both a conscious and unconscious desire to live forever. This is one of the main reasons why people who are unable to conceive are frequently so frantic to have children, and when the defect is irremediable, turn to adoption. They are generally not conscious of their true or basic motivation. Simple observation must tell them that children are a lot of work, a great deal of trouble, and that the raising of them is quite costly. It is also obvious that children represent a great loss of personal freedom, require personal sacrifices, and frequently add stresses to the marital situation. While the conventional reason for adopting children is that they are an essential part of life, the truth of the matter is that consciously or unconsciously most people cannot bear the thought of their life terminating in oblivion. It is not uncommon for bachelors and old maids, as well as married couples, to adopt children; sometimes they even adopt other adults, with the proviso that they change their name to that of their adopting parents. As long as a child lives they feel that part of their self will survive. Since most adopting parents are not aware of their true motivations anyway, they maintain the fiction that adoption is equivalent to having a natural child. Those who are consciously aware of the fact that they desire immortality, will generally not adopt.

There are, of course, men and women who actually are conscious builders of a dynasty and who want to have as many children as possible so that the family name and enterprise, whether it be a kingdom or a business, can be carried on in perpetuity.

One of the most common ways of attempting to attain immortality is the building of a monument, which can run the gamut from the monolithic pyramids of Egypt to a modern foundation. Philanthropists' endowments frequently take the form of a university chair or building or hospital wing which bears their name. If their body cannot live, at least a substitute, in the form of a name attached to an academic chair or a shaft of marble, can remain to remind someone that once upon a time there was such a person who existed and lived. The planning and erection of a monument provides solace while still alive, and helps perhaps to assuage the fear of death in some measure to those who can afford it.

Man also attempts to perpetuate himself through work, fame, and money. Instead of money being a by-product of work, both work and money frequently become ends in themselves. Instead of working to live, how frequently we see the spectacle of those who work to die. Many men work to the exclusion of everything else, including love, play, creativity, human relationships, and even to the ruthless exclusion of the things they like to do most. Many of these men would claim that they are working to make a fortune so that they can retire. Many of them run so hard because work and money have come to them to be synonymous with life itself. Whether this common syndrome has its etiology rooted in infantile insecurity or in the cultural values of society, this type of man is not working to live but rather to die. This is the man who works night and day, until he has his stroke or coronary. The twin motives of work and money are interwoven.

Work becomes a surrogate for life itself and all that is human because it is strongly reinforced with money itself or the expectation of money. Work also becomes a refuge and anodyne from personal and human problems that one dare not confront and that one is unable to solve or resolve. One becomes accustomed to work, comfortable with business or professional associates, is screened from personal problems, and in addition to money, receives such secondary rewards as power and recognition from his occupational activities.

It is rather obvious that in our American culture the father is frequently regarded as a rather pathetic figure, and one only has to see how he is portrayed in such comic strips as "Blondie" and on TV soap operas to confirm this. Yet this same "joke" or ineffectual being is frequently a driving businessman or professional whose sole function in life seems to be to make enough money to support his family and former families in luxury, so that his wife and ex-wives can have cocktails and luncheons in expensive restaurants, his children can go to the best schools, and they can maintain memberships in exclusive country clubs. The cream of the jest is that he himself does not have time to enjoy these facilities or to acquire the athletic skills necessary to use them. Nor does the money or luxuries he showers upon his wife and children result in their loving him more, but paradoxically, rather less. He is frequently resented for his devotion to his work or business, which his family, quite accurately, feels indicates a preference for work rather than their company. Of course, the more they show their resentment, the more alienated he becomes and the more he tends to lose himself in his work; it then becomes a vicious circle where he in turn resents and hates them for being ungrateful beneficiaries of the way he truly is "killing himself." So his work becomes a passion and an end in itself, and the more he loses himself in his work, the less he thinks of his life, its purpose or meaning, and his mortal nature.

Man works for many reasons not the least of which is to live. But would he work so hard to live if he were fully conscious of the fact that he must die? Man frequently works to the degree that he does, not so much because he has to, but because he does not know what else to do. Work becomes to him ultimate meaning and reality. But does not man really work because he feels he is forced to, rather than because he wants to? Would he not rather play? And, once he finds himself working, does he not convince himself that his work is very meaningful and all-important? We see the case of the man who works to the exclusion of everything else, including all human relationships. He convinces himself that he has found ultimate meaning; he works night and day and perhaps forgets that he must die and that he and his work may be completely meaningless. This is the man who has completely forgotten his mortality, and in his headlong flight to escape it, is really rushing to embrace it. This is the man who kills himself, finally, after first killing everything in himself that is human. This is the man who suddenly dies in his middle years after having achieved, or being on the verge of achieving, great material success. This is also the "success" who one fine day puts a bullet through his head, the day he suddenly remembers what he has been so desperately trying to forget, the fact that he is a man and mortal. This is at the exit point of his life, when he realizes that he has been alienated from an authentic existence by pursuing false and inhuman goals, and in their pursuit, he has sacrificed his life, alienated his family and friends, and lost his opportunity for happiness.

Whether man loses himself in work for work's sake or for money, it is much the same effort. He convinces himself that work or money have ultimate meaning, and he devotes himself to the pursuit of his holy grail in his effort to forget what he knows all the time to be true, that it really doesn't make very much difference what he does and that he must die in the end anyway.

Then there are those men who spend a lifetime searching for something meaningful to do and trying their hand at many different things; but these people suffer from the delusion that, if they find the right activity, they will be happy and find the answer to their problems. While there is no question that a man will frequently find one form of work more fulfilling and congenial than another, these people do not realize that they are looking for ultimate meaning and certitude; they too are fleeing from the truth of their own finitude. Let us now look at some of the specific fears that comprise man's fear of death, and begin with his fear of losing time.

3

The Fear of Losing Time

THERE ARE different kinds of time. There is biological time, as measured by the menstrual cycle or the aging of the body; chronological or clock time, which is measured by watches or other measuring instruments based on the movements of the earth, sun, and moon, or other cyclical processes; and psychological time, which is how man thinks about and relates to chronological time. Psychological time, which includes the category of relative time, is the species of time with which we are principally concerned. The relativity of time is best exemplified by the familiar example of a toothache as contrasted with an evening of love-making. Five minutes of a toothache seems like an eternity, while a night of dalliance seems like but an instant.

Newton conceived of time in two main categories. He considered absolute, true, and mathematical time as something that flowed "equably without relation to anything external, and by another name is called duration." He defined what he called relative, apparent, or common time as "some sensible and external (whether accurate or unequable) measure of duration by means of motion, which is commonly used instead of true time; such as an hour, a day, a month, a year."

Newton's definitions also point up the important caveat of not confusing the measuring unit, i.e., the clock, with the phenomenon to be measured, i.e., duration.

The tyranny that time exercises over man may be traced in large measure to this very confusion between the measuring unit and the phenomenon to be measured. Another source of confusion has been the thinking of time as an *entity* or *thing*, rather than as a process or phenomenon. Whatever real or absolute time is, it is what we are attempting to measure with our devices. As man has increasingly been able to perfect his measuring devices, make them more and more precise and capable of measuring intervals as brief as a billionth of a second, so he has increasingly confused the phenomenon to be measured with the measuring unit. In truth he does not know what time really is, even as he perfects ever more accurate timing devices, which are analagous to the rulers with which he measures space. However, as he continues to be able to subdivide time, so he believes that he can constantly accomplish more and more in any given time period.

When we think of time, we normally think of watches and clocks ticking away the passage of seconds, minutes, and hours. We think of time like sand running through an hourglass, forever running freely until the glass is turned no more. We think of time as something that we cannot grasp slipping endlessly through our fingers. The apparent movement of time casts a pall over all man's activities. It permeates, with a sense of urgency, everything he does. From his birth until his death he is hurrying to keep pace with it. (It should be stated that we are writing here primarily about Western man. However, as the influence of the United States upon the rest of the world proceeds apace, what we write is becoming increasingly true of the condition of Eastern man as well.)

Modern man is concerned more with saving time than his soul. Since time cannot be stored up or hoarded, he attempts to compress it. He attempts to accomplish his tasks in ever shorter time intervals. The Industrial Revolution was based upon the concept of turning out more and more product in less and less time. Time and motion studies have as their chief object the mechanization of man. Automation is the result of the realization that machines are faster, more efficient, and make fewer mistakes. The replacement and obsolescence of man inevitably follows the desire to accelerate everything. The classic comic-film sequence parodying the attempt to mechanize man was portrayed by Charlie Chaplin in *Modern Times*. Chaplin is a factory worker on an assembly line; his job is to tighten nuts on a fast-moving production line with a wrench in each hand. He can barely keep up with the belt, and when his work is done for the day, he walks around still tightening imaginary nuts with nonexistent wrenches.

The saving of time has become an obsessive preoccupation, if not a mania. It has also become an industry as time-budgeting diaries and other time-saving devices are marketed; they purportedly enable man to manage his time more efficiently, compress it more effectively, and accomplish more and more in less and less time. For many years a leading correspondence school ran a famous advertising campaign which showed a man working late at night by the light of a lamp. The copy for the ad read "While Others Sleep." Here was an advertisement which appealed to the widespread guilt that is felt over the misuse of one's time. It suggested that, while others wasted their time sleeping, here was a man who was forging ahead by night study which would reward him richly in the future. Man's obsession with the desire to put every moment to effective and productive use is also seen in the devices which are marketed to enable man to learn as he sleeps. Even though these devices are nothing more than automatic clocks attached to phonographs, and their efficacy has yet to be validated scientifically, they have great appeal to those who feel that they are wasting their time sleeping.

Work, which has as its result the earning of money, has always been considered the most socially approved use of time. In fact, this is the key Protestant ethic developed by Max Weber in *The Protestant Ethic and Spirit of Capitalism.* Consider the anomaly of the situation. Man has more and more leisure time to spend because a 70-hour work week has already become a 40-hour week; a 30- or 25-hour week is not too distant; in fact it is already here in some industries. Man will have more and more time in which to do less and less, and to feel increasingly guilty about wasting time. We shall see an even further increasing number of moonlighters who hold two full-time jobs, and we suspect that the motivation will not always be purely monetary. The idea that man must always be engaged in something "productive," and productive to most people means an activity that produces money, is so firmly rooted that when men retire, they frequently suffer from a loss of identity and self-esteem, a shock which frequently precipitates a coronary or a stroke.

How frequently the parent tells the child, "You are wasting your time." The implication is that there are pressing things for them to do, and goals to reach. And to a great extent this is true, as there is always homework or some other project that must be done. It is always assumed that time is for accomplishing something, getting somewhere, and making money. It is rarely considered that time may be for something else, like living and the enjoyment of life. All such goals are dismissed as the ambitions of a playboy, dilettante, fool, or wastrel. Living for joy is permissible only when the work is done, the money made, and we have earned our two-week vacation in the sun, during which we are supposed to live and have fun. The businessman must frequently justify his sailing or golfing on the grounds that it is necessary for his business. Nor is this deceit just for the benefit of the Internal Revenue Service. It is true self-deceit as well, because he feels guilty about doing anything that is not related to making money. In many cases the eagerly anticipated vacation turns out to be a disenchantment, and the return to the job is a relief from the failure of reality to live up to what had been so eagerly and long anticipated.

Man regards clock time as something outside and apart from himself. All of our devices for the measurement of time nurture the illusion that it is quite independent of us and flows along "equably" like "Old Man River." As man matures he learns that events occurred before he was born, and in all likelihood, will take place after his death. He learns this from people and books that antedated his birth. He realizes that people who lived before are now dead, and assumes that people will live after his death. So time to him becomes something like the movement of the earth and other astral bodies. It goes its own way and he can do nothing to affect its "equable" and inexorable flow.

Man, as a result of both his arbitrary division of what he calls time into segments and his identification with clock time, has become a teleological creature who postulates for himself an equally arbitrary beginning, middle, and end. Birth is normally thought of as the beginning, and death as the end. Man regards as his beginning the earliest point of his existence that he can clearly recall, and death as the point where he loses consciousness forever and his ability to recall or project. As we have learned from hypnosis and psychoanalysis, man has the capacity to recall infantile memories of which he is no longer conscious. Thus, he finds that he had a previous life and existence of which he is not conscious. There are people who are amnesiac and suffer from a fugue; this has been defined as a pathological disturbance of consciousness during which the person performs acts of which he appears to be conscious, but of which, on recovery, he has no recollection.

The teleological conditioning of man has a sinister effect on his entire life. He has postulated a static world and invented a yardstick which measures change in relationship to it. He uses this measuring instrument not only to calculate the duration of his life, but as something that governs the very conduct and quality of it. Once he arbitrarily postulates that three score and ten is the proper length of one's conscious duration, and that death is a terminal point, everything is endowed with a sense of urgency as he rushes against a relentless time clock or ruler, which exists only as a product of his own conceptual process. Man individually attempts to save all the time he can, and collectively spends much effort and money on medical research, which has as its goal the extension of man's life span through the eradication of disease and prevention of illness.

Much of what man does is goal-oriented and directed to the accomplishment of certain objectives which he desires to achieve before reaching the terminal point of his life. He must obtain an education, he must be successful in the world, he must marry and raise a family, and finally, he must provide for his old age. While the knowledge of his eventual death hovers over everything man does, and even conditions it, his whole life, as he actually lives it, represents a flight from confrontation with his ultimate destiny.

But what do we most fear about time? If we are frightened and tyrannized by the ticking of our clocks, do we not now see they are simply measuring devices we have converted into a ruling tyrant? Are we not aware that we are not guaranteed any fixed period of time in which to accomplish certain things, or to live? Is it not true that our life, as we know it consciously, may end at any moment, and without warning?

Time is simply a series of thoughts related to, and based upon, other thoughts, and founded upon notions that do not accord with the way things are. The future is a speculation based upon past experience. Both the past and the future draw our attention away from the experience of that which *is*, the eternal here-and-now.

But it may be argued, does not a thought exist? Yes, it does, but it is also transient and evanescent and frequently misleading, as in the case of our thoughts about time. When a notion, which is an illusion, is permitted to persist and become an obsessional *idée fixe*, it has the capacity to confuse and direct our attention from what *is*. What we have done is to take an idea or thought that has a certain utility, such as in arranging to meet someone at a certain time and place, and permit it to become an external and illusory reality that tyrannizes its inventor and creator. Time then is nothing more than an arbitrary convention of the thought process which we consider as the mind. The division of time into measured intervals by mechanical devices serves to further the illusion that it is something we are using up as reflected in the expressions *tempus fugit* and "time is a-wastin'." The only thing that is flying and "a-wastin' " is our own mind, which is little more than a series of rapid and successive thoughts.

Suppose we computed the average number of paces a person takes during his lifetime, and suppose we were conscious of that fact, rather than the number of years the average person lives. Let us further suppose that the sum is determined to be one hundred million steps. Even though we would realize that it is just an average, we would focus on that average figure and believe we were *entitled* to that number of paces during the course of our lifetime. This would make us very conscious, would it not? of how many paces we were taking, whether each one was strictly necessary, whether we could perhaps take longer ones, and finally, how many we had left. And when we reached our allotted number of paces, we would feel as though we were living on "borrowed paces" rather than "borrowed time." We would feel that every pace counted, and mothers would tell their children, "Don't waste your paces," rather than, "Don't waste your time."

If we were so conditioned, we would all wear pedometers instead of wrist watches and would become conscious of every stride. The analogy is an imperfect one, and we will stretch it no further. The point, however, is that the fear we have of wasting time is based on an arbitrary measuring device created by our own intellectual apparatus. If we measured our lives by paces rather than minutes, we would obviously not be so frightened by the Frankenstein creation we call time; instead, we would take it for granted, as we now do our locomotion. We are now unconscious of how many steps we take during a day; if we measured life by our paces, we would be just as unconscious of the passage of seconds, minutes, and hours. We can measure our life in any number of ways. As J. Alfred Prufrock said, "I have measured out my life with coffee spoons."

* T. S. Eliot, "The Love Song of J. Alfred Prufrock," by permission of Harcourt Brace Jovanovich, Inc.

4

The Fear of Decay, Irreversibility, and the Unknown

UNLIKE TIME, most decay is something that is only too visible, tangible, and has odor. We see decay all around us in the form of rotting carcasses, crumbling structures, and refuse. We see maggots and flies swarming over the bodies of dead animals, and recoil at the stench of decaying fish or garbage. From a strictly scientific viewpoint, however, there are of course exceptions: rust has no odor; beta decay is not visible; and all "decay" is not negative, as in the case of fermentation. Some commentators on death have tried to make a virtue out of necessity, and have attempted to obtain consolation from the fact that the body in a state of decomposition supports more forms of life than it does before death. Jean Finot in a quaint book* written around the turn of the century describes in vivid detail the various insects that inhabit the corpse, and takes a negative view of cremation on the ground that it interferes with the cycle of nature. This sort of cosmic philosophy is of the same order

* *La Philosophie de la Longévité,* Paris, Felix Alcan, 1906.

as that of the mystic who feels that he is contributing to the nitrogen cycle every time he answers a call of nature. The "companions of our graves" like the "beautiful fly *stabulans*," the "brilliantly metallic green *Lucilia*," and "the charming butterfly of the genus *Aglossa*" can offer consolation only to the aforesaid mystic. The spectacle envisioned by Finot is exactly what man fears most about death, the disintegration of his body providing a host for the worms.

All is transiency. If we are going back whence we came, why fear it? The answer, perhaps, is that death is of the future and represents something we can fantasy about, and fear is always of the future. One moment we see someone walking, laughing, and living, and the next moment he is dead. It is both frightening and inconceivable that the same thing is certain to happen to us one day, when we will be the "other person."

A great Zen master, possibly Bodhidharma himself, was once brought before an emperor who asked him, "Who are you?" He replied, "In truth, my lord, I do not know." This is considered as one of Zen's most profound utterances. There are three things, like the identity of one's mother, of which we can be truly certain or truly uncertain: we do not know who we are, where we came from, and where we are going. Nothing can be more vain than to speculate on these three riddles and to hope to come up with an answer. The only possible answer to these queries is, "In truth, my lord, I do not know."

Of what can we be certain then? It is perhaps the beginning, and end, of wisdom to realize that we cannot be truly certain of anything. But it is at least possible that we may return to our original state, of which we know and can recall nothing. We can be certain that we are transient, and like everything else, will eventually disintegrate. The Old Testament states it: "Dust thou art, and unto dust shalt thou return." Lucan writes the same thing in a slightly different form: "The earth takes back everything which it has brought forth." While much, including this book, has been written about death, thus far we just don't know what happens when death intervenes.

But is this any reason to attempt to console ourselves with fables and fairy tales? The bedtime stories are not all consoling either. The happy kind are all reminiscent of Marc Connelly's Negro musical comedy *Green Pastures*, where God is pictured as a benevolent and all-powerful elderly man who works at an old-fashioned rolltop desk in an office. The angels sit around on fleecy clouds, in white bedsheets, twanging banjoes and harps, and planning a great big fish fry in the sky. The other myth depicts an after-life of everlasting hellfire and brimstone, where we shall roast endlessly for our earthly sins and transgressions. This myth has been used by the priests from time immemorial to frighten their flocks into conforming with whatever code of conduct they sought to impose.

Perhaps more to the point is the fable of two twins chatting in the womb before their birth. One says, "I think I'll stay here. It's nice and cozy, and God only knows what it's like outside." The other twin says, "Maybe you're right, but I'm curious about what's out there." One of the points made by this tale is that the twins in the womb are in the same position as we are with regard to our fear of death. Their interior world is all that they know, and they can only speculate on what will happen after leaving the womb. So can we only guess what lies ahead of us. Assuming that the child is better off after birth, so it is possible that we may be better off after death. It is possible that our life is simply a preparatory step for an evolutionary destiny about which we know nothing. It has been suggested by such authors and dramatists as Jean Paul Sartre, Franz Kafka, and Samuel Beckett that what we call life is really hell. It certainly is a hell for many people whose only releases are chemical adjuvants (such as alcohol and opium) which act as anodynes and enable them to forget their conscious existence for a brief period of time. Even the most favored of human beings, in terms of social, material, and artistic endowment, frequently find life to be largely suffering. Buddha, of course, said life *is* suffering.

But another point generally overlooked in the anecdote about the twins is that they have no choice, just as we have no choice when it comes to facing death. Since it is the order of all things, and since it may presage an existence that is infinitely better than the one we now "enjoy," then why fight it? We fear and resist it because we feel it represents an irreversible state and the unknown.

It has been said that going to sleep is like dying, and if man is not afraid of falling asleep, he should not be afraid to die. While it is true that we could die in our sleep and never awaken, we always feel that such a possibility is something, like death itself, which happens only to the "other person." So when we go to sleep, we anticipate waking up and we know that it is not an irreversible process. Based on the law of probability, it is assumed with confidence that we shall awaken after we have lived through our sleep as the "dreamer." In death, we believe that we will dream no more.

What we are fearful of in death is its apparent irreversible nature; it is so final and permanent. The normal consolation proffered as an antidote to the finality of death is the endless cycle of life and death, which suggests that death is anything but certain, and that the cycle of all life in nature is birth, death, and rebirth. As Cornford, the distinguished historian of ancient philosophy, wrote: "Further, the life of Nature in the cycle of the seasons follows the same curve as the life of man. Nature, likewise, has her phases and grades. Her life waxes in spring, culminates in summer, and in autumn wanes again, till her fruits decay and leave only the seed, which must be buried in death, and lie in hope of resurrection. The year with its two seasons of light and dark, warmth and cold, drought and wet, corresponds to the two halves of man's life-circle."* Hippodamus the Pythagorean said much the same thing: "All mortal things, by necessity of Nature, revolve in a wheel of changes. . . . When they are born they grow, and when they are grown they reach their height, and after that they grow old, and at last perish. At one time Nature causes them to come to their

* F. M. Cornford, *From Religion to Philosophy*, New York, Harper & Row, Torchbook ed., 1965, p. 166.

goal in her region of darkness, and then again out of the darkness they come back into mortal form, by alternation of birth and repayment of death, in the cycle wherein Nature returns upon herself."

Plato in his *Politicus* described souls as seeds which fall into the earth before each new birth. The Greeks believed that the earth is the source of all life, and that the souls of animals and men, as well as plants and trees, spring from the earth. The Greeks believed in a basic soul-stuff which could pass at one time into a man, and at another into a plant or animal. It is not necessary to elaborate here the Greek concept of soul or the imperishability or immutability of soul-stuff. It is sufficient to recognize that the Greeks' observation of the cyclical aspects of nature was the basis for many of their philosophical and religious beliefs, which in turn have had such an enormous influence upon our own thinking.

The cyclical phases of nature are self-evident. Observation tells us that everything is part of an eternal process which repeats itself endlessly. Nothing is in a condition of stasis, least of all man. All of nature is part of an endless cycle of birth, growth, death, and rebirth. Nothing comes to a dead end.

But the aforesaid consolations are really not reassuring to anyone except perhaps some mystics. Man is not consoled by the cycle of nature and the analogies to plants and seeds. Nor is he reassured by the knowledge that new fruit will grow and there will be others born after him. His main concern is that *he* will die and not live again in the form he now knows, and that his self or "I" will perish for all time.

This is why the resurrection of Jesus, in the human form which his disciples and apostles knew, was so all-important to the growth of Christianity. It represented a fulfillment of man's deepest desire not to die, or if die he must, to be reborn in the same form and with the identical self and "I" that he and others previously knew.

5

The Fear of Life—
The Pain of Living

THE PURPOSE of this chapter is simply to attempt to demonstrate what is perhaps obvious. A good part of our life consists of pain and suffering and is expendable; man would gladly relinquish this portion in favor of nonexistence or what he commonly regards as death. Why then should man fear death, the absence of feeling, which in many cases he regards as preferable to life, which consists of sensation?

Of course, in what follows there are many borderline cases. Much of what man would give up in exchange for nonexistence, he would only be prepared to surrender temporarily. For example, very few would be willing to give up life to get rid of a toothache or headache. However, where there is no surcease possible from intolerable pain, many would prefer death to the intense sensation that continued living entails.

The further purpose of this section will be to lead the way for the succeeding chapters, where we will attempt to show what it is that man does *not* want to give up, at any cost, and what he regards as synonymous with, and vital to, his existence. These are primarily his pleasurable physical and mental sensations and his anticipation of renewing and experiencing them again and again.

Obviously, we do not mind giving up all psychical and physical suffering, pain, and anguish. It is apparent, is it not, that much of what we call life is suffering, as Buddha suggested. We certainly would be delighted to give up the possibility of experiencing any intense future physical pain, whether as a result of an accident or illness. Physical pain is perhaps the most dreaded of all human experiences, and even though it can be controlled to a great degree by anesthetics, there are pains so severe that they can be relieved only by drugs that cause loss of consciousness. These palliatives are generally derivatives of morphine which are physiologically and psychologically addictive when used in large doses or over a long period of time, and the drug can become more of a problem than the pain which it was originally employed to relieve.

Physical pain, as in certain terminal cases of cancer, can be so great that patients literally beg for death, for what they desire most is an absence of the intense sensations that are torturing them. Intense pain scientifically employed by such masters of the art as the German Gestapo can drive people insane as well as cause death. The inhuman techniques employed by the Nazi sadists were designed to inflict a maximum amount of pain while still keeping the individual conscious. But no one would argue with the proposition that man would gladly give up that part of his future life comprised of intense physical pain, whether it be of a variety just described or the anguish of a bad toothache. If a man had a choice of living two more years, pain free, or four more years, racked with pain, is there any doubt that he would choose the briefer span? In the example referred to earlier to demonstrate the relativity of the passage of time, a brief period of sharp pain is an eternity contrasted with the brevity of a much longer period spent making love.

Physical pain, however, unless someone is particularly unfortunate, occupies a relatively small period of the average lifetime. Memory of pain, like other unpleasant phenomena, is rather quickly repressed and forgotten. We probably, however, have more pain and illness during the course of a lifetime than we commonly realize, if we were to total all headaches, stomachaches, toothaches, and operations. As the tempo of our lives accelerates, and as the "stress" diseases proliferate and become more prevalent, more people suffer more and more pain from common psychosomatic illnesses like migraine and ulcers.

This leads us to the psychical disorders such as anxiety, depression, and neurosis. There can be no question that the incidence of these illnesses is also waxing. With the possible exception of headache remedies and other analgesics, more drugs are sold to relieve depression and anxiety than for any other single purpose. These drugs are swilled in the billions of doses by millions of sufferers all over the world. Statistics reveal that during 1966 one out of every two prescriptions written in the U. S. was for a drug that affects the mind; thirteen billion units of amphetamines, barbiturates, and tranquillizers were produced, or seventy-two for every person.

Those who have suffered from any real form of anxiety and depression would gladly reduce their life term if they could bar these psychic twins from their life. The reason we would gladly reduce our life span by the time we have lived in intense physical or mental pain is obvious. When we are depressed, anxious, or in pain, we are not enjoying life. When we are psychically anguished, we cannot really function adequately, and sometimes not at all. Migraine sufferers, and many millions suffer periodic attacks of this common ailment for a good part of their lives, are rendered *hors de combat* from life by this illness when it strikes. They must withdraw for many hours or a few days, generally to a darkened room where they attempt to sleep it off while drugged with medication.

Much of our life is consumed by mental anguish and suffering and dark despair and unhappiness. Psychic pain can be the product of either mental factors or physical conditions—or a combination of both. Depression can be triggered by both physical and mental events, as in postpartum depression, which is a psychiatric ailment which frequently afflicts women after childbirth. There are very few families who have not been touched by this kind of suffering as a result of one of its members having a mental disease. With all the chemical advances that have been made in the chemotherapeutical treatment of psychic illnesses, the institutions that treat these unfortunates are still overcrowded, and there is a steadily increasing imbalance between the number of patients and the number of psychiatrists and psychiatric nurses available to care for them.

Life is a series of changing aspirations which are frequently frustrated and rarely attained. Much of our life is characterized by disappointments of one kind or another. We are constantly disappointed in people, love, and career; and many of these disappointments result in bitter and long-lasting unhappiness.

It is a common personal phenomenon to see a person turned "bitter" or "sour" because of a failure to reach a coveted rung on the ladder of business, politics, or academe. What does the common expression *he has soured on life* mean? It means, does it not? that the person has become chronically unhappy, pessimistic, and miserable, and that his entire life has become overlaid by gloomy feelings and thoughts that are reflected in his actions and speech and by his facial expressions and bodily postures. We see the spectacle of someone who has "resigned from life and is just playing out his string."

But what must be the innermost feelings of the person who feels he has failed in his major life endeavor? Has not the salt lost its savor for him, and has not the sun ceased to shine? Is not the most beautiful warm vernal day, dank and dark for such a man? Does not the remainder of such a life become a curse which is unmitigated by much joy? Can any imagined hell be worse than such a life? We have all experienced brief periods in our life when we have felt this way. Can we imagine what it must be like to live this way for the rest of one's life with no exit, save one? And is not this exit sometimes chosen by those who have progressed from anxiety to depression, to deep depression, and finally, to death itself through suicide?

The business of getting along with people, including the members of one's own family is also productive of much pain and suffering. How much pain is suffered from, and inflicted upon, those we supposedly love most? How much anguish is suffered from friends, coworkers, and employers, and how much suffering is inflicted upon them? Without analyzing the reasons for all human conflict, does not a large measure of it derive from insisting upon the primacy of one's own will and seeking to impose it upon others? In the current idiom, do we not frequently attempt to prevent others from "doing their thing," or do we not tell them what we think "their thing" should be?

Untold personal suffering results from trying "to make it" or to succeed in life. How much unhappiness and anguish results from just trying to survive and to take care of one's family? Survival to members of an upper urban society in San Francisco or New York has a rather different meaning than survival to a poor family in Watts or Bombay. "Making it" for many still means getting enough to eat and a place to sleep. Even in the United States, and even in San Francisco and New York, many live on the narrow ledge of physical survival and are still beset by the difficulty of securing the basic commodities of food, shelter, and clothing.

But let us look at just some of the more common varieties of love. Some psychological experiments with rats, which measure their motivation by requiring them to cross an electrically charged grid, have shown that the maternal drive is the strongest of all the basic instincts with primacy over even thirst and hunger. Paternal love is commonly recognized not to be as selfless as maternal love, but both parents are generally presumed to love their children dearly.

Yet with the possible exception of sex, more time is logged on the professional listeners' chaise longues discussing conflicts with parents than any other single subject. No relationships, with the exceptions of marriage and sexual relationships, cause so many problems or so much heartache. While we do not intend a thorough treatment of the child-parent relationship here, the origins of the strife should be pointed out. The child wants all of the parents' love, all the time. The effect of siblings on this demand is only too obvious and too apparent. It is doomed to frustration which leads to rage and anger against the sibling rival as well as the parent. The anger directed against the rival frequently turns to physical aggression, as we all can testify from actual experience or observation. The motivation is simply the desire to destroy or injure a rival who is competing for a mother's or father's love. Rage and anger directed towards a parent frequently represents a child's effort to reach the parent and to claim the parent's complete and undivided attention. A tantrum alarms the parent, and as he tries to calm the disturbed child, it forces him to bestow upon the child what he or she craves most, or at least a symbol representative of it, the parent's total love.

Child brutalization and physical mistreatment are very common; and one has only to read the daily newspapers to confirm this sordid and distressing fact. Children all over the world are injured, permanently crippled, and killed by cruel and sadistic parents. Many children and infants who are brought to hospitals for treatment of injuries due to an accident or fall have in reality been victimized and battered by their parents. Interns and emergency rooms have long been able to recognize the physical stigmata of a beating, as opposed to a fall, and to pierce the thin veil of a parent's cover story. We are shocked when we read about insects or animals that do not care for their young and even eat or devour them. How much more shocking are the numerous such cases among human beings.

The psychic suffering caused by child-parent relationships is much greater than any pain suffered as a result of physical maltreatment. Enormous anguish results from having children who are subnormal or who are victims of either accidents sustained at birth or during life. Aside from the economic burden imposed by such tragedies, the personal suffering caused to a parent by a sick or malformed child can only be fully appreciated by those who have borne similar burdens.

Case histories of traumatic relationships between parents and children proliferate throughout psychiatric literature. The very nature of the relationship is responsible for much of the conflict and trauma. The parents' task is to assist their children's growth, development, and maturation. During infancy, the total helplessness of the child requires that he be taken care of totally. The theory is that control and supervision are gradually relinquished until the child can take care of himself and control his own existence. The theory, however, breaks down in actual practice. The parent confuses his true role with the feeling that he owns or possesses his child. He confuses the fact that he has brought the child into the world and assumed his support with the notion that the child must do everything he says and must be a puppet responsive to the strings he holds in his hand. The parent is confused by the fact that his wooden Pinocchio has somehow become a real live boy with drives and ambitions and a life of his own. He is unable to relinquish control, and this is the source of much of the difficulty that arises between parents and children. The simple point is that the relationship between parent and child, which ideally should be one of love, is frequently one of rage, anger, and hate. A relationship which should be serene is very often tumultuous and stormy. A relationship which ideally should be friendly and helpful many times turns into the jagged rock upon which the ship of life is impaled. How great is the pain and suffering caused by this intimate relationship which should be loving and benign!

There is only one relationship which is theoretically more loving than that between parent and child, and that is between husband and wife or sexual lovers. This is the most intimate relationship in life. It not only involves, in the case of marriage, sharing one's life, but sharing the very peak experience of life itself. Other sexual relations, such as those between homosexuals and lesbians, also involve the sharing of a unification experience, but without the marriage compact that is theoretically for life. In practice, however, it turns out to be somewhat less, since one out of four is the current statistic on the marriages which founder and end up in the divorce court. Of all human relationships, there is none that can turn to hate so quickly as that of a sexual partnership that has gone awry.

The only relationship which can sour as quickly from love to hate is that which exists between men who are engaged in the pursuit of money together. The reason why the love and business relationships turn to hate and curdle so quickly is basically the same. As long as the relationship works and is viable, we feel secure and sense that we are being cared for in one of life's most vital areas. Since our greatest impulse is to be loved and to be taken care of completely, and since this need exists from the time we have emerged into a hostile world, it has assumed primacy in our personal hierarchy of needs and values, whether instinctual or learned.

Money is a learned value and need, but one which becomes more and more potent and important as time goes by. The reason money becomes so all-important is that it is necessary to the satisfaction of all of our other material needs, including physical survival itself. In a success and material-oriented society, it has become the quintessential symbol of achievement and has assumed a motive force so great that it has a powerful effect on the physical and sexual potency of man.

It is difficult to weigh on balancing scales the pleasure and pain one gets from sex. There can be no question that it can be the source of man's most exquisite mental suffering as well as physical pleasure. Sex is further complicated by the twisted mental involutions that lead to sexual sadism and masochism, wherein man derives sexual satisfaction and pleasure only as a result of beating or being beaten. There is also the phenomenon known as psychic masochism which describes a condition wherein man derives pleasure from mental suffering and torment, of which sex produces its fair share.

While the beating of wives and mistresses is more widespread than most people realize, let us concentrate on the mental pain suffered in marriage and in sexual relationships in the name of love. Is the psychic pain we inflict upon one another in an average marriage even conceivable? From our earliest sexual stirrings, sex causes much confusion; and from our birth, the need for love becomes a source of pain insofar as it is unrequited. As we have seen, the demand and concomitant need for love is insatiable, and once it becomes interwoven with sex, we have a most powerful combination of motivational forces. This demand persists from birth to the very end of life, and as man matures sexually it becomes ever more powerful and insistent. Insofar as it is constant, it can rarely be permanently assuaged or satisfied, and at best it is, like hunger or thirst, only satisfied momentarily. Again, a distinction must be made between sexual love and the more diffuse need for care, loving concern, and physical protection.

What about the simple inability to get along that in some degree afflicts marriages and parent-child relationships? Quarreling, arguing, verbal sparring, and fighting is to a degree symptomatic and characteristic of all family relationships. This type of chronic verbal conflict is wearing, painful, and gives rise to much anguish, and yet it is a permanent aural background of many unhappy lives. Can we doubt that the overwhelming number of marriages that endure are basically unhappy? Is it not true that many so-called enduring marriages are characterized by bitter conflict and only persist because of economic inability to disengage; lack of alternatives; age; illness; or an agreement reached, by the parties to the marriage contract, to disregard its pledges and to go their separate ways.

We may arbitrarily divide the emotional and psychic aspects of marriage as well as life itself into three categories: pleasurable, painful, and neutral. Obviously sexual relations and physical love are moments when we are most aware of physical sensations of pleasure, assuming that there is a satisfactory sexual relationship between the partners. Psychic traumata are prevalent in sex when the partners are not suited to and do not satisfy each other. Frustration at this level leads to general acrimony, dissatisfaction, and eventual dissolution. Assuming, however, no such antagonistic situation exists, the sexual moments are perhaps the most physically pleasant we experience in marriage or in a love relationship.

A good part of our life falls into the neutral category, when we go about it in a routine fashion, working, eating, and sleeping. We are generally conscious of neither pain nor pleasure during such periods, except perhaps when we have an exceptional meal or are successful in accomplishing something extraordinary. But how much of our conscious life is filled with anger and annoyance at events and at others? How much time is spent in arguments and in either trying to impose our will on others or in defense against others who seek to impose their will upon us?

Is it not a fair conclusion that life is predominantly suffering and neutral rather than pleasurable? Is this not particularly and increasingly true as one descends the socio-economic ladder? The rich can amuse themselves with the games, toys, friends, and sexual partners that money can buy. But even these pall eventually and no longer continue to amuse as the shadows of life lengthen and the affluent are confronted with the hard problems of life, including death, serious and chronic illness, conflict with children, loss of sexual potency, mental illness, and the psychic and physical concomitants of aging. If one could construct a balance that would weigh the moments of pleasure against both the neutral moments and the time that we suffer from disease, or psychic or physical distress, can there be any doubt about which would tip the scale? Certainly the happy times are as a few grains of sand as compared with the Sahara of pain and suffering or apparently neutral activity.

Without going any further into what is neutral time, we may arbitrarily define it as those periods during which we are not conscious of either pain or pleasure. Is not much of neutral time, perhaps, suffering which we do not recognize or refuse to admit? Much of neutral time is composed of periods during which we block out of consciousness our actual suffering, by work or play or by simply refusing to think about it, and attempt to forget and to lose overselves in such distractions as movies, books, parties, theater, other forms of entertainment, work, charities and "good works," and politics.

While physical and mental suffering are different, are they not both torment, and would we not do everything in our power to rid ourselves of these afflictions? Even the knowledge that time will bring surcease, and the awareness that "this too shall pass," is of scant consolation to one who is on the rack of psychical or physical torture. Would we not be cheerfully willing to relinquish from our life span several times the duration of the actual time we spend in acute suffering, if we could only be free of pain?

Much of what passes for life is not only neutral, as we have defined it, but is actually a boring, uneventful existence. Most people just exist, suffer, or struggle, and their pleasure is obtained negatively rather than positively. It is obtained not by real joy, but by anesthetizing themselves to the suffering that is real life. For example, alcohol makes us feel better by making us less sensitive to the impingement of physical reality and less aware of our own troublesome thoughts. It is an anodyne, like narcotics, that renders us oblivious to our troubles for a brief period of time by raising the level of our sensitivity threshold.

We have attempted to establish what we feel is a rather self-evident point: if life is not all suffering, certainly a great deal of it is. We have also attempted to make the rather obvious point that man would gladly relinquish that portion of his life that consists of psychic and physical pain, which varies from individual to individual. We have further attempted to point out that much of man's time is neutral time in which he is conscious of neither pleasant nor unpleasant sensations, and of course, a quarter to a third of his life is generally spent in sleep. And even in his sleep he has nightmares! So what man is really afraid to lose, is he not, are his pleasant sensations which actually occupy a rather small part of his life. The nature of these pleasant sensations and their relationship to death will subsequently be examined. Before we do so, however, let us look at man's great fear of losing his self and his ability to think.

6

The Fear of the Loss of Self and the Cessation of Thought

THE FEAR OF THE LOSS OF SELF

There has rarely been a word or concept in the entire body of psychological and philosophical literature that has produced more confusion. This confusion is further compounded by the use of such terms as the real self and true self, as opposed to the pseudo self. Let us examine the concept of the self and the origins of the fear of its loss.

The New Testament states in Matthew 10:39: "He that findeth his *life* shall lose it; and he that loseth his *life* for my sake shall find it." This celebrated paradox is repeated in almost the same words in at least three other places.* It is our opinion that *life* is being used synonymously with the concept of *self*, as normally used and even as employed in the New Testament. This seems to be confirmed by two equally well-known quotations. In Luke 9:25, the New Testament states: "For what is a man advantaged, if he gain the whole world, and lose *himself*, or be cast away." Here

* Matthew 16:25; Mark 8:35; Luke 9:24.

we see the introduction of *self*, which is used in preference to *life* appearing in the passages previously cited. In Matthew 16:25, we see still another synonym employed for *life* and *self*, namely, *soul*. This passage reads: "For what is a man profited, if he shall gain the whole world, and lose his own *soul?* or what shall a man give in exchange for his *soul?*" (Emphasis in each quotation is mine.)

While there are undoubtedly earlier references in Western literature to the loss of one's self, here we see in the New Testament some early uses of the concept of self and its synonyms. We also see expressed in the last quotation the origins of man's fear or concern over the loss of his self, and we see spelled out the opinion that even if one were to gain the whole world, it is nothing compared to the loss of one's soul, life, or self.

A great deal of the Indian and Oriental literature deals expressly with the doctrines of the self, true or real self, and false or pseudo self. The meaning, however, of these terms in this literature is equally murky and confusing and produces much misunderstanding. It is our purpose to attempt to clarify the meaning of the term self as well as the variant concepts of real or true self and pseudo or false self. We shall also examine the concept of self to clarify what man really fears losing when he is afraid of losing his self, and through this clarification, to illuminate and understand the relationship between the fear of the loss of the self and the fear of death.

Not only is the self at times synonymous with life and soul as used in the Bible, but it is also the referent when we say "I" or "me." Many philosophers and psychologists have attempted to define the self. It is not our intention here to review all the various theories and definitions of the self, although we will make reference to some of them. Anyone interested in a definitive critique of the various Western theories of self, up to the time of his writing his book, should consult William James.* He discusses each of the principal theories of the self in what is a classic of closely reasoned analysis and interpretation. But our interest, as was James's, is to inquire what is the self; how do we know it; and why are we afraid to lose it.

Let us answer the last question first. If we have associated life with both soul and self—and if we have been taught that, even if we gain the entire world, it is vain and empty because we lose our self or our soul—should we not dread its loss? When we think of our self, we think of it in terms of its being a conglomerate which is our essence; it is therefore natural to fear its loss. What could be more reasonable than to fear the loss of the self which we regard as a combination of our mind, our body, and everything that makes us unique?

And in fact it is a conglomerate and is so defined by James as follows:† "*In its widest possible sense*, however, *a man's Self is the sum total of all that he* CAN *call his*, not only his body and his psychic powers, but his clothes and his house, his wife and children, his ancestors and friends,

* *The Principles of Psychology*, New York, Dover Publications, Inc., 1950, Vol. I, Chap. 10, "The Consciousness of Self."
† *Ibid.*, p. 291.

his reputation and works, his lands and horses, and yacht and bank-account."

James divides the constituents of the self into two classes. One class consists of (*a*) material self, (*b*) social self, and (*c*) spiritual self; the other class constitutes the pure ego. James's material self is made up of the body, clothes, immediate family, property, and material possessions. He defines man's social self as "the recognition which he gets from his mates," and says that "a man has as many social selves as there are individuals who recognize him and carry an image of him in their mind." By spiritual self, James means "man's inner or subjective being, his psychic faculties or dispositions, taken concretely."

Most people, at least in the West, although many in the East as well, would regard as their self the material and social self described by James, Mead,* and others. This is the self that may be described by a man's material possessions and the opinion others have of him as well as his own opinion of himself. Man's opinion of himself, as well as the opinion of others, is based to great extent on his material possessions. This is particularly true in the West, where the familiar wisecrack echoes through the land, "If you're so smart, why aren't you rich?"

Suicide furnishes a significant clue as to what man regards as his essential self. If we examine the circumstances surrounding suicide, we can see what man regards as im-

* *George Herbert Mead on Social Psychology*, ed. Anselm Strauss, Chicago, The University of Chicago Press, Phoenix Edition, 1965, Part VI, "Self."

portant enough to give up his life for. In the East as well as the West, the social self in the form of "face" is all important. Loss of face is the trigger of many suicides. Loss of face in Japan can run the gamut from the failure to win a war, which caused many suicides among the high- as well as low-ranking Japanese military leaders, to the failure to pass examinations, which causes many suicides among Japanese students annually. Loss of face causes many suicides among other races as well, but in the West, loss of face is most frequently related to loss of wealth, which in turn is a factor of social standing. The important element in loss of face is what others think of oneself; this affects what one thinks of himself. Insofar as man regards himself as a person who is essentially a cluster of materialistic possessions and social traits, the loss of those traits and assets is sufficient in many cases to precipitate the assassination of his faultless physical body; he finds life insupportable if others cannot regard him in the way to which he has been accustomed.

The frustration of physical and sexual love is another frequent cause of suicide. Here too it is the social self which is in jeopardy. Someone is jilted and becomes a suicide because he cannot endure knowing that his self has been rejected and that he is no longer loved and adored. He cannot live with the notion that he is no longer the idolized focus of the other. So what is important here, as it always is when the social self is involved, is the opinion of the other.

There are of course many social selves. They are not only as numerous as the people who know the individual, but they are as numerous as the individual's own concepts of himself. We also have as many social selves as those we come into contact with. Even within the same family or business organization we have different selves depending upon whether, for example, we are relating to a spouse or child or to a superior or a subordinate.

The idea of the multiple selves we possess is touchingly expressed in *Dombey and Son* by Dickens, when the Captain thinks Walter has been drowned at sea.

"He wasn't my flesh and blood," said the Captain, looking at the fire—"I an't got none—but somewhat of what a father feels when he loses a son, I feel in losing Wal'r. For why?" said the Captain. "Because it an't one loss but a round dozen. Where's that there young school boy with the rosy face and curly hair, that used to be as merry in this here parlour, come round every week, as a piece of music. Gone down with Wal'r. Where's that there fresh lad, that nothing couldn't tire nor put out, and that sparkled up and blushed so when we joked him about Heart's Delight, that he was beautiful to look at? Gone down with Wal'r. Where's that there man's spirit, all afire, that wouldn't see the old man hove down for a moment, and cared nothing for itself? Gone down with Wal'r. It an't one Wal'r. There were a dozen Wal'r that I knowed and loved, all holding round his neck when he went down, and they're a-holding round mine now."

We have many selves, many of which we relinquish quite naturally as we mature, grow, and progress in life. For example, the self of the kindergarten child yields to the self of the grade-school pupil, and so on and so forth, until one finally completes his education and becomes still another new self. There are those who do not relinquish an old self that would normally be shed as part of the maturation process. There is the familiar example of the university student who receives his diploma but never graduates. This is the old grad who, no matter what he may do in life, still clings to his undergraduate self. Although his postgraduate involvement may take the form of alumni activity, he basically cannot give up the self he created in college and cannot give up the life that "late he led."

It is apparent that we have and develop many selves during the course of our life. Some we may relinquish naturally, while we cling to others because we have found them to be particularly satisfying, like the aforesaid successful undergraduate or B.M.O.C. (Big Man on Campus).

There are those selves that we are only too anxious to relinquish. Suppose a man has been a bankrupt or failure in a particular business endeavor and then perhaps goes on to achieve success in some other position. You can be sure that he will rarely think about, and scarcely recall, the self that was he when he failed. This self is buried and forgotten, and if he ever recalls it, it is as though it all happened in a dream.

We are afraid most of all to lose the self that we are currently most identified with; we regard this self as our permanent self. Even though it is evident that our permanent self is subject to change (or to changing events, as the selves of the German Jews were shattered by the growth of Nazism), we tend to regard our present social self as permanent and to forget the many selves we have discarded and others that are likely to be born or created in the future.

In short, what most of us regard as our self is nothing permanent, but is merely a constellation of changing thoughts orbiting around a physical body and relating to a certain number of people with whom we are in contact and involved with in certain activities.

Thus, it should be apparent that the self we so zealously cling to is not permanent, but evanescent and changing by its very nature. We slip so imperceptibly and gradually from one self to another that we are rarely aware of the variety of selves that compose our lives unless we look backward from the vantage point of hindsight. Certain aspects of our self may harden early and become relatively permanent and immutable throughout all the other changes of the self. For example, notions regarding one's religion, politics, and social class may become adamantine and remain constant throughout one's lifetime. The idea of "face" may also become a permanent part of one's self. Depending upon the society, certain of its characteristics may be more fixed in one than another. There has been traditionally far more mobility, both financially and socially, possible in the West than the East.

Among the more immutable aspects of the self, there is the physical body. As in contradistinction to the changing thoughts that comprise the self, the body is relatively permanent even though it goes through the cycle of birth, growth, life, death, and disintegration. While our social self may change, we are always aware of our body as unique, and barring disease, accident, or death, relatively stable and permanent. So, however, we normally regard our self or the changing selves. According to James's theory of the pure ego, whatever self was ascendant at any particular point in time would appropriate to itself all of its past thoughts and therefore former selves. Even though it is apparent that the social self changes as one develops, we tend to regard the social self (primarily what others think of us and we think of ourselves) almost as permanent and as unique as our body, in spite of all the empirical evidence to the contrary.

This is a point which produces a great deal of confusion. While every physical body is different, as illustrated by finger prints, palm prints, teeth, and voice prints, so is every social self. Everyone has had different relationships as well as a different body. The important difference is that the body remains relatively stable, and we do not normally identify with it when we think of our self, but rather we tend to identify with the constituents of our social self. The social self, however, is a rapidly changing phenomenon. Another illustration of this is falling in love. It is obvious how our life and self changes through love or infatuation. When we fall in love, our thoughts primarily revolve around the other person and what he or she thinks or feels about us. A new self has been born overnight. What one person thinks about us has suddenly become the most important thing in the world, and what everyone else thinks about us has just as suddenly become relatively unimportant.

Now let us turn to James's thoughts on the pure ego and his conclusion that "thought itself is the thinker," to which he attaches the concept of the appropriation of all previous thoughts. It is doubtful if anyone, including the Zen

Buddhists, will ever have the last word on the complex question of what constitutes the real self or the essential identity of man; nevertheless, there seems to be agreement among all those who have considered the matter most deeply that thought itself is the thinker. There are other theories that can explain, equally well as the appropriative theory, what the connecting thread is that constitutes the link between thoughts, including some views that are based on computer theory as well as on the current scientific search for the memory molecule. As we have seen, man consciously and unconsciously throughout his lifetime relinquishes various selves that he has elaborately constructed. While he can give some of these selves permanence, they are in fact as impermanent as the endless fluctuation of thought. As we shall see, what man fears losing is the very process of thought itself, which unlike the changing selves is not impermanent, but is constant and—as James said—is the "directly verifiable existent." Man's primary and basic identification is not with his rapidly changing thoughts, but with thought and the process of thought itself. What happens when man ceases to identify with his thought process will be seen in the subsequent chapter "Life and a Theory of Unification."

Mere repetition of a thought does not give it any more substance than any other thought, except as it appears to the individual who thinks it and who confuses familiarity and frequency with reality. How powerful—and therefore how real to the thinker—these thoughts can become, is apparent in the suicides which we discussed previously. If one really sees and understands that any one particular thought has no more reality than another, then what is one left with, and what is the self? Is James's pure ego—the "passing thought," the only "directly verifiable existent," the sum of all previous thoughts that were "me"—is this the "bodily existence"? Much of man's basic confusion surrounding the understanding of the self has stemmed from his regarding it as an entity rather than nothing or "no thing." What happens if one "lets go" and realizes that the self is nothing more than a rapid succession of thoughts, many of which may be incorrect, inexact, and unrelated to any objective reality? It is possible he may then feel as though the ground has been cut from under him and that the rock on which he stood has turned to quicksand. What he thought of as fixed and eternal is now realized to be ephemeral and evanescent. He hopefully realizes that his self changes from moment to moment; that he can affect or alter his self; and that it is nothing more than a kaleidoscope of rapidly shifting and changing images and thoughts. Where now is the self that man is so fearful of losing?

We have just seen that the essence of the self that man fears losing is thought, so let us now look at how he fears the cessation of thought itself.

THE FEAR OF THE CESSATION OF THOUGHT

One of the chief components of our fear of death is the unconscious fear of the cessation of thought. It is unconscious in the sense that it is rarely articulated: when we contemplate death, we hardly ever think of it in terms of losing our power to think, but we rather think of death as signifying the end of the bodily existence with which we are familiar.

While we are alive, however, we are rarely conscious of our bodies when there is no physical pain or exertion. Even when we are using our bodies in sports, walking, or in other physical activity, we are almost never aware of the movement of our hands, arms, legs, feet, and the wonder of it all. An exception, of course, is athletes who are trained to be aware; but most of us are not so trained, and when we walk with others, we talk, and when we walk alone, we think many different thoughts. This is illustrated by a well-known Zen story. A Zen master was asked by one of his disciples, "Do you ever make any effort to make contact with truth and reality?"

"Yes, I do," replied the master.

"What do you do?"

"When I am hungry, I eat and when I am tired, I sleep."

"Isn't this what everybody does and can't they be said to be doing what you are doing?"

"No."

"Why not?"

"Because when most people eat, they do not eat, but are thinking of many other things, thereby allowing themselves to be disturbed; and when they sleep, they do not just sleep, but they dream of a thousand and one things. This is why they are not like myself."

Most of our life is lived in our mind. Without thought

what would we be? We regard a person who cannot think as a vegetable and not a human being. Regardless of whether the etiology is functional or organic, persons suffering from such a disorder are consigned to the refuse bin of life. They are confined and forgotten in the dreary ward rooms of hospitals for the insane until death, which sometimes is encouraged prematurely, intervenes. The physical functions of the body, in the case of mental defectives, are frequently unimpaired, and these human vegetables frequently outlive more normal people. As a matter of fact, the severely mentally disturbed patient has a remarkably low incidence of disease compared to the rest of the population.

Whether we realize it or not, we identify not only with our thoughts, but also with our entire intellectual apparatus. The distinction between thoughts and intellectual apparatus or thought process should be clarified. What we mean by a thought may be words, such as, "I will buy a new necktie," or "I want to see the new play that just opened." A thought may also be simply a picture or an image, like a thought of someone's face or a painting that one has seen. In other words, we think in both words and pictures, sometimes separately, but generally in combination. For example, when we think, "I will buy a new necktie," we may also "see" a tie that we had previously noticed in a shop window. We of course may also think in numbers or in some other symbolic form, as we do when we engage in abstract reasoning. Dreams too are a form of thinking. In dreams we generally dream in pictures or a combination of words and pictures. We probably also dream in words and abstract symbolism, as witnessed by the many who have solved scientific and mathematical problems while sleeping.

What we mean by thought process or intellectual apparatus is slightly more complex. It is clear, is it not, what we mean when we suggest not being attached to any single thought or series of thoughts. We simply mean the recognition that one thought has no *more* reality than any other thought. For example, we cannot touch or handle a thought. The nature of thought is for each thought, almost instantly, to be superseded by another. It is like a string of Chinese firecrackers where each one sets off the next. When we talk about thought process and intellectual apparatus, we are talking about the continuing on-going process and phenomenon of thinking rather than any single thought or even group of thoughts. It is the sequential nature of thought itself to which we refer. Henri Bergson's analogy to the motion picture is still the best metaphor. On a strip of motion picture film we see a series of slightly differing still shots. When these, however, are projected on a blank screen we see moving people, process, and the phenomenon of continual action. There are two realities, one is the individual stills and the other is the motion picture as projected. The underlying reality is the series of stills; but when man thinks of a motion picture or sees one, he does not think of the true nature of what he sees. This analogy could be developed at much greater length. Perhaps it will suffice, however, to make the distinction and the point.

The Fear of the Loss of Self

It is relatively simple from the foregoing to understand the reasons why we should not be attached to any single thought. It is of a much more complex order to detach oneself from the entire process of intellection. The reason, as we will attempt to show, is that man identifies almost totally, not just with his thoughts, but also with his thinking process and discursive intellect. He cannot conceive of himself as a "thought-less" person. Krishnamurti reiterates, "The word is not the thing." The thought is not the thing either. Nor is the person the thought. Nor does the sequential nature of thought, like the projected motion picture on the screen, give it any more reality. If we are not the thought, we are not the thoughts, nor the process of thought, which is simply one thought succeeding another in our "moving" picture.

Without our thoughts we fear we are nothing, which we are, but we are afraid to let go of them even for an instant. There is another Zen story that illustrates this point. Two friends were walking along a mountain road and observed in the distance a lonely man standing on a ridge. One of the men said to the other, "I wonder what he is looking for?" The other replied, "Perhaps he is looking for a lost sheep." When they reached the man, one of the two men asked him if he was looking for a lost sheep. He answered, "No." The other man then asked, "Perhaps you are looking for a friend?" And again he replied in the negative. One of the two companions then inquired if, perhaps, he was just admiring the view, and again he replied, "No." One of the two frustrated companions then asked, "If you are not looking for a lost sheep, or a friend, and you are not admiring the view, then what are you doing?" The solitary watcher on the hill replied, "I'm just standing." The point might even have been better made if the question had been put, "If you are not looking for a sheep or a friend, and are not admiring the view, then what are you thinking about?" And then finally, "If you are not looking for a sheep or a friend, and you are not admiring the view, and are not thinking about anything, then what are you doing?"

Most of us are afraid just to stand—we must be either thinking constantly or channeling inputs into our sensory system via our ears, eyes, or body. Many of us are even incapable of being alone with our thoughts. A common spectacle is a person walking along the street with a transistor radio appended to his ear. These are people who are perhaps fearful of their own thoughts and are uncomfortable unless certain inputs are periodically being made into their sensory system. Some people need and demand an injection of multiple sensations, as in the case of a football fan who is watching one game while listening to several others, eating peanuts, drinking beer and smoking—all at the same time.

All of this is by way of illustration of the point that people are afraid *not* to think. Most people think that meditation is concentrating on, and thinking about, one object or thought. This is only preliminary to true meditation, which is *no* thought and *no* thinking. It is hard enough for most neophytes and apprentice Buddhas to concentrate on one thing at a time without requiring them to cease all thinking and all thought. Many spend a lifetime meditating and never get beyond the point of being able to keep their focus on a single object or an idea for a slightly longer period than when they started. Most are terrified of *not* thinking, and most of us are slaves of our own thinking apparatus and thoughts. There is perhaps nothing man fears more than the cessation of his thoughts, which is his mind. Breaking his attachment to his mental apparatus is perhaps the hardest thing in the world for man to do, but perhaps the most vital if he is to change, flower, and become a new being.

Death represents a cessation of all thought; this unconsciously terrifies man. One of the arguments frequently made by those who would make a contribution to the elimination of the fear of death is that we should not be afraid to die since death is a form of sleep. Aside from the fact that we fully expect to wake up when we go to bed, we know sleep does not mean the cessation of thought. What else are dreams but thoughts clad in symbolic form? Even when we cannot remember them, we know we continue to think in the form of dreams in our sleep. Death, however, means no more thoughts, no more thinking, and no more life. Without thoughts, man would regard his life as no life and insupportable; he would feel consigned to a vegetative existence which has no value, and in most cases, he would prefer death.

But what if our real life, rather than the life of the mind, is vegetative? What if it can be shown that what man values most in his life are not his thoughts, but his vegetative nature? What if it can be shown that one of man's deepest drives is to stop the process of thought and to cease to think? What if it can be shown that what man thinks he fears most is really a consummation that he deeply desires? If this can be shown, then man can perhaps begin to lose his fear of the cessation of thought because he will realize that his deepest desire is for that state which comes into being when his thought totally ceases.

And now let us turn to man's fear of the loss of his pleasures.

7

The Fear of the Loss of Pleasure

Confucius said, "Until we know what life is, how can we know what death is?" We cannot properly investigate death unless we examine life, particularly where death is defined as that which begins when life ceases. We are now living in the dawn of the age of vital-organ transplants which has raised anew the question as to what constitutes clinical death. But we do not have to dance on the head of a pin and make fine clinical distinctions in order to determine what is life. Life, as we commonly think of it, is a combination of feeling, loving, thinking, seeing, breathing, acting, eating, drinking, tasting, sleeping, moving, waking, talking, procreating, hearing, and smelling. While we can live without seeing, walking, smelling, tasting, and procreating, insofar as one or more of these functions are subtracted or abstracted from our lives, so we feel that our lives are diminished to some degree. But few of the things which we regard as essential to living are really necessary to sustain man's vegetative functioning.

While man can derive pleasure from those things which are necessary to maintain and sustain physical life, he draws a distinction between living and existing. Existing to him constitutes the operation of the simple vegetative processes of eating, drinking, sleeping, breathing, etc. Man is, by and large, as unconscious of his vegetative existence as he is of the automatic functioning of his autonomic nervous system, and he takes it for granted. Only when he attempts to transform existence to living, is he at all conscious of it, as he is when he develops a taste for a certain kind of food and anticipates the joy and pleasure of consuming it. Eating then becomes living rather than existing. So it is with the other vegetative functions that can be transformed into experiences of living rather than existing.

The agent of transmutation is the thought and memory process which selects certain physical experiences that have been felt as pleasurable and seeks to repeat them. The constant repetition of physical sensations felt as pleasurable is, of course, the process of conditioning. Certain physical sensations are virtually universal in their appeal. In spite of its allergenic properties, the enjoyment of the taste of chocolate seems to have such widespread appeal. The pleasing qualities, as in chocolate, tea, or coffee, may be inherent in the substance itself, insofar as it creates pleasurable somatic experiences, or it may be as a result of other factors of a psychic nature which accompany the ingestion of the food or drink. Suppose a mother feeds her child sugared-oaties with hot cocoa. The chances are that a very strong conditioning bond would be created in the resulting symbiosis of mother love, sugared-oaties, and cocoa, and a lifelong addiction would result. Every time the adult eats his oaties and cocoa he is not simply existing, but living and reliving the wonderful days of his infancy when his mother so lovingly cared for and fed him.

So many of our vegetative experiences are transformed from virtually unconscious functions to highly conscious activities that we learn to associate with what we regard as real life or living, as opposed to simple vegetative existing, which we hold in contempt. This is why certain eating establishments become so important to many. The natural function of eating becomes interwoven with compelling social factors, like the importance of being seen in the right place, with the right people, and at the right time.

While strictly speaking it is difficult to classify sexual activity as a vegetative function, since it is not necessary to sustain and maintain the life of an individual, it is perhaps on the borderline, and its proper functioning seems necessary to the physical as well as psychic health of mankind. Nevertheless, it furnishes another example of a natural function that has become revalued and transformed into an important part of living rather than of existence.

Our literature, our contemporary communication media, and our advertising—all combine to reinforce the prevalent notion that the enjoyment of sex is the chief purpose of life. Since sexual life and sexual attractiveness have become so important, everything connected with sex becomes living rather than existing. We are living when we go out on a date with a member of the opposite sex, however remote actual sexual relations may be, and whether or not they ever take place at all. When this living is reinforced and combined with the living of dining at a fine establishment, then we have a heady combination and constellation of forces which have nothing to do with the actual act of sexual intercourse other than comprising a part of the ritual dance which hopefully will lead to the experience itself.

Man also feels that he is truly living when he affirms himself egotistically as a unique, separate, and distinct human being.* He may feel that he is living when he receives recognition for something he has accomplished, whether it be a promotion or a Nobel Prize. He feels he is really living when he is caught up in a great enterprise, whether it be a political campaign, a social cause, or a profit-making venture. Anything that man feels truly passionate about gives him a heightened sense of participation in life. Then he feels he is really living, as opposed to merely existing, which he denigrates as "just vegetating"; he just does not feel that merely existing is doing anything significant or particularly important. Just existing seems shameful somehow and a waste of time when one should be living. Man founders on the notion that he must affirm his egotistical uniqueness. How often does a mass murderer give as his excuse his desire to make a name for himself? The fear of anonymity and of being nothing is so great that people will even kill to affirm their ego and to assuage the

* Hubert Benoit, *The Supreme Doctrine,* New York, The Viking Press, Compass ed., 1960, Chap. 4.

accompanying anxiety which comes into being as a result of regarding oneself as a nullity or a nonentity.

Actually, the whole point of life may be mere existence; man's basic problem in terms of his unhappiness and alienation may be his feeling and thinking that he should be something more; that he should be doing great things; and that he should build a mountain. His curse may be the ambition to be unique.

If man examines his life, he can see what it is he likes to do best and most, and what activities he finds most satisfying. If he makes a content analysis of his own thoughts, he can also see what it is he thinks about the most. He thinks most about those things and activities that give him his greatest pleasure. There are times when the thoughts of man are largely occupied by a besetting problem, and he is unable to think of anything else. But when man is not so troubled, his thoughts turn to the things he enjoys most, and of course, sex leads all the rest, at least for most of us.

Most people think of things that they find pleasant—they anticipate pleasures as well as relive them—and most of all, they have dreams. The male dreams of girls, food and drink, sports, parties, money, success, and plans for leisure time. Women dream of the same things, but in addition, think more about marriage, clothes, hair styles, and fashion than does the male of the species. Unmarried women also think of marriage, and to a greater extent than does the bachelor. Men however have recently become increasingly interested in the things that have in the past been more or less predominantly of interest to the female.

But why do man's thoughts particularly and primarily revolve upon these things rather than the myriad of other notions that might occupy his mind? It is because, while engaged in these activities, he spontaneously encounters unification states during which he is most alive and happy. Paradoxically, these states do not occur when man normally feels—or rather, thinks—that he is living, but when he is existing purely on a vegetative level. Man normally feels that he is living when he can intellectualize about it. But the essence of the unification experience is the spontaneous halting not only of specific thought but of the very process of thought and intellection itself, as well as a loss of self.

8

Life and a Theory of Unification

A THEORY OF unification previously propounded by the author* and restated here holds that the mainspring of man's behavior, and his basic motivation, is to attain and repeat the spontaneous peak experiences in which man is unified with himself, others, and the world, and in which his thought process, his thinking, and his discursive intellect are momentarily stilled.

We are "happy" when, however briefly, we become one with ourselves, others, and the world of nature. It is in this state that all of the layers of egotistical affirmation and the self that we have so carefully nurtured drop away for a split second in time. What results is an experience of intense being and feeling of oneness with the essence and principle of life itself. The intellect, whose true purpose has been perverted, ceases to maintain the mind-created split between subject and object, where the object is everyone and everything out there, including oneself. Man is no longer

* *Self-Love*, New York, The Macmillan Company, 1970.

an object to himself. It is not only the subject-object split itself that man finds so intensely disturbing, both on a conscious as well as unconscious level, but the fear that results from this split, where everything and everyone out there are regarded as hostile to his self and as a threat to its existence. Once insight is gained into the unification experience, it can be seen that *what man has depreciated so thoroughly as mere vegetative existence is really the state in which he comes into his own true nature and attains oneness and happiness.*

Man leads a life of self-deceit through which he views the world darkly. He views life through strata of overlays which reify many thoughts that are nothing but egotistical affirmations. For example, as we have seen in our discussion of the fear of loss of self, all men have a feeling of uniqueness which starts with their body and includes their name, social status, occupation, education, etc. This reification process creates feelings of self-importance and self-esteem. Anything that enhances man's own favorable opinion of himself adds to his egotistical affirmation, and anything that detracts from it diminishes it.

A man can live his entire life by the reification of certain ideas, thoughts, or notions relating to social status. Let us suppose that Van Rensselaer Pierpont III is like Hilaire Belloc's Godolphin Horne, who "was nobly born and held the human race in scorn." He sees the world as a place where social status is all and would dismiss an Einstein or Lincoln if he were not enshrined in the *Social Register* or the *Almanach de Gotha*. This is the man who regards social acceptability as all, bases his life upon it, and regards as success the affirmation by others of his own egotistical notions of his identity. Such a person is cut off from all humanity. He is not aware of the primary essence and identity of all human beings and all life; he is not aware that he has chosen a life based on the reification of a few ideas which have no more reality and tangibility than any random thought that crosses his mind during the course of a day, such as, what tie to wear when he goes out. Since his exalted notion of his own social status gives him maximum ego gratification and egotistical affirmation, he is constantly seeking to satisfy its insatiable demands.

But this is the kind of man who, like Richard Cory in the poem of the same name by Edward Arlington Robinson, can suddenly see that he has been living with falseness, emptiness, unreality, and self-deceit; he can go home "one calm summer night," as did Richard Cory, "and put a bullet through his head." This kind of man can also one day encounter a powerful experience of unification so strong that he will drop the deceits of a lifetime to pursue and repeat the same unification experience. As we shall see, while the unification experience is the same, regardless of the activities that produce it, there is a hierarchical order in terms of the depth, strength, and intensity of the experience. Heterosexual orgasmic experience is probably the peak unification experience open to most men and women. The orgasmic experience encountered in the sexual relationship is so powerful, and the satisfaction so profound, that everything else seems trivial and unimportant, particularly when it is uncontaminated by psycho-social problems of sexual adjustment.

Sex, however, is only one of the activities that produces these experiences. Powerful unification experiences can occur spontaneously in all of the areas where man finds pleasure. It is precisely because certain activities produce unification experiences that he prefers them to others. What he savors is not the activity, but the unifying experience itself and the dropping away of self.

In addition to man's other activities that we have catalogued, let us look at a few of the other things that man likes to do. He likes to be entertained by drama, films, comedy, music, and dancing. He likes to read books, magazines, and other literature. He enjoys dancing, singing, and laughter. Can it be doubted that man enjoys rage, anger, fighting, and even war? Can it be doubted that man enjoys the spectacle of man combatting man, animal against animal, and even animal versus man? Man has always enjoyed the hunt, and perhaps to a lesser degree, fishing, and has even found war, killing, and revolution greatly satisfying. Public executions and hangings provided great entertainment not too long ago. The circuses of Rome have been unrivaled in the history of man in providing organized entertainment in the form of bloody spectacles; thousands of men and women were killed in organized mock battles, individual gladiatorial combat, and in warfare between man and beast. Remnants of these barbaric entertainments may still be seen today in boxing matches, cock fights, bull fights, wrestling, and certain contact sports like football and rugby.

It is believed that most of these activities can be explained comprehensively and understandably by the author's theory of unification. We have discussed what unification is; so let us now look briefly at its mechanism and how man unifies. Unification is a coalescing of mind and body with nature so that they and we are one. It is a stilling of the mind, a condition of no thought, and a momentary ending of our identification with the discursive intellect and thought process. It is in effect a mystical state of brief duration and low order. It is characterized in retrospect as being a state of oneness, happiness, elation, excitement, intense feeling, or orgasm. What has happened in a negative sense is that, in a split second, all of the encrusted layers of egotistical affirmation constructed by the discursive intellect have fallen away, and the identification with the thought process, which is the discursive intellect as well as the false self, has been shattered.

Before the climactic, orgasmic moment that characterizes the experience, there has been a buildup of tension which is both of the mind and the body. When the mind thinks about sexual activity for more than a few moments, the body responds. The single best and most vivid example of the effect of the psyche on the soma is the erective state that ensues in man when he turns his thoughts to sex. A similar condition in woman is the hardening of the breast nipples when she is sexually aroused. As the mind thinks more and more about sex, the body responds by reaching a physical state of tension. As the mind dwells more and more upon an activity which is productive of a unification experience, other thoughts drop away in favor of the titillating thoughts that stimulate and excite the soma. The mind thinks fewer and fewer thoughts as the body responds, and physical and psychical tension increases to the point where there is no thought and finally an orgasmic explosive resolution. It is at the point of the orgasm itself that there is no thought, no mind, no body, no thought process, and in the vernacular, "no nothin'."

This analysis is applicable to all the other unification experiences whether consciously or unconsciously induced. Let us look at what we commonly regard as a *negative* experience, the familiar state of rage or anger. The very ordinariness of this emotion might seem to indicate that it is a poor example of unification. However, the point of using this common feeling as an illustration is to show that man can be unified even under circumstances not ordinarily associated with peak experiences of pleasure. We are all familiar, are we not? with the condition of rage and anger, and how a minor and innocuous remark can trigger a more acrid rejoinder, which in turn results in an accelerating quarrel. Voices are raised, tempers flare, and bitter and wounding remarks are made. These quarrels can destroy lifelong relationships of marriage and friendship, and finally, and not infrequently, culminate in an exchange of blows, the use of weapons, and even murder. No more substantiation for this is needed than the police statistics which reveal that family quarrels account for the single largest category of homicides.

What happens then during a quarrel or argument and

when we are angry? While we are primarily interested in the unification stage that *is* rage or anger, it is necessary to analyze the condition precedent. One of the most common causes of quarrels and arguments is a contradictory remark which can also be expressed by intonation, attitude, or gesture. It can be a contradiction of a statement of fact or of an opinion. The apparent contradiction that actually starts a quarrel may simply be the manifest or symbolic representation of a more basic underlying and latent conflict. Beneath the surface may be the eternal conflict between man and woman, husband and wife, or parent and child. For example, suppose a man is sitting home on a Sunday morning reading the newspaper; and let us suppose, further, that the wife announces that they will visit her parents after lunch. He may have had absolutely no plans for the afternoon and ordinarily may have been quite amenable to visit his in-laws; but responding to more than the words or the content of the suggestion, he may be angered by a dictatorial and peremptory manner or tone, and he may reply angrily, "The hell we will."

Before we look at the galloping escalation that proceeds apace, let us examine the more underlying conflicts. Perhaps the marriage in question has endured for some ten years or more, and perhaps the husband is enamored of another woman or would simply like to be. Perhaps he would like to be free to do and to come and go as he pleases, even if it is just to pursue a hobby like golf or sailing or to watch a football game on television. Let us suppose, further, that he feels that his wife and his children prevent him from doing what he really wants to do. Obviously, when his wife makes her fatal announcement, as though Jehovah himself had spoken, all of the simmering resentments erupt to the surface, and the cold war becomes hot.

There is an even deeper layer of conflict, and that is the conflict between man and man, which is based upon the fundamental notion that he is separate. This premise causes him to regard all others as basically hostile and as a continuing threat to his existence. No matter how apparently benign the relationship is, we are all aware of how quickly love can curdle into hate. While a comprehensive discussion of this important aspect of human relationship is not too germane here, it may be suggested that unless man's desire for love and care, which stems from the fear of his finitude, is constantly nourished, the relationship may turn sour if he begins to feel his existence is threatened.

But let us return to anger and see what happens in the process of getting angry. Before we become angry what we call our minds function in what we may call a normal mode. That is, many ideas flit through our minds as one thought is quickly succeeded by the next. There is no consciousness of any particular emotion. A remark is made which triggers an angry response. What has happened in the brief interval between the first remark of the wife and the angry response of the husband? All of the slumbering resentments have come rushing to the fore in the form of the enraged retort. Almost simultaneously with the reply, a physical response also ensues, additional adrenalin is poured into the blood stream, the voice is elevated, the eyes flash, the tachycardia is increased, the muscles of the face and jaw tense. First we have thought angry, and then we begin to feel angry. As we feel angry, we begin to think increasingly angry, and so on and so forth, until thinking literally almost ceases and finally does come to a standstill in the orgasmic climax which can range from a shriek, to the slam of a door, to a blow, or to murder. The parallel to the buildup of sexual tension is exact. Body responds to thought, and thought to body, as the unification process enfolds, until mind and body coalesce in the ultimate orgasmic blow-off. As the process develops, it is increasingly difficult to interrupt by thought since the essence of the experience is no thought and the total cessation of the very process of thought itself.

We have postulated as man's primal and most powerful motivation and instinct, the drive for unification. Heterosexual orgasm is probably the unification experience *par excellence*, followed by homosexuality and autoerotic unisexuality in that order. In addition, however, man achieves spontaneous unification experiences in many of his other activities, sports, hobbies, music, art, and poetry as well as laughter and anger. In many cases man may obtain unification satisfaction in only one way, and this particular activity may consequently assume great importance, albeit unconscious, for that reason. For example, let us take the case of a middle-aged man whose wife is chronically ill and unable to engage in sexual relations. Let us further assume that for cultural, ideological, or personal reasons he has no other sexual outlet of any sort. We can readily understand that in a normal man this state of frustration would alone be sufficient to cause a chronic state of irritability that could easily erupt into a full-blown frenzy. But whatever the cause of the rage, it is possible it may become his sole source of a unification experience since—again for reasons of age or other physical condition or indisposition—other activities, like dancing, sports, and creative work, which normally produce unification experiences, may not be available to him.

To continue our analogy, is there not a period of calm which follows a temper tantrum that is similar, if not identical, to the enervated state of peaceful lassitude which is typical of the postcoital condition? If anger is a man's sole opportunity to be unified, he is conditioned to become, and be, angry frequently. But he does not know why he is such an angry man. He is frequently not only contrite, but terribly concerned about his destructive behavior; thoughts of contrition and remorse proliferate as he emerges from the state of unification, and the thought process begins its inexorable and automatic operation once again. It is frequently at this point that he, heaven help him, is sometimes motivated to seek the services of a psychoanalyst.

When participants are asked why they are involved in sports with a high degree of physical risk, they generally reply that they do so for the "kicks" or thrills or because of the challenge. The classic response given to the question *Why climb a mountain?* is *Because it's there.* In many sports, such as Grand Prix racing and mountain climbing, it is frequently only a question of time before a serious or fatal accident occurs, and yet the athletes continue to persist and compete. It is self-evident, in the light of the foregoing analysis, why they continue to compete and participate in such dangerous sports. The more deadly the sport, the greater the tension, and the more satisfying the orgasmic climax—whether the race is won or lost, or the summit is reached or not. In the words of the legendary gambler Nick the Greek, next to "playing and winning," he liked "playing and losing." What racers and mountain climbers savor, like gamblers, is the unification experience, and they seek those activities where they can enjoy maximum satisfaction by prolonging the tension, by increasing the degree of risk even to the extent of putting their lives on the line, and by attempting to extend the orgasmic climax itself. It may not occur to them that they can obtain the unification experience without risking their lives. The reason for their choice may be that their source of unification experience is more extended in duration than in any other activity they know.

Most people are totally unconscious of the mainsprings of their motivation and are at a loss to explain why they do certain things, particularly acts considered to be unsocial or self-destructive. Once it is seen that man's deepest drive is to achieve the unification states that he now accidentally achieves, it can be understood why he persists in certain behavior patterns even though they are self-defeating, self-destructive, and even degrading. The sufferer's anguish may be exacerbated by the fact that he is confused by the objective activity, such as, drinking, narcotics, sex, or criminal activity, and thinks that they are what he enjoys. He totally misses the main point that it is not any outward activity, whether it be social or antisocial, that he enjoys; his satisfaction derives from an experience that is not of the mind or of the body, or even both in combination.

If a man's chief source of such experience is from any of the antisocial activities above, he can only be weaned from them if he can achieve similar satisfaction from some other source. So before we seek to deprive someone of the sole source of his experience of unification, or ask him to voluntarily relinquish it, it must be replaced with something of equal value that provides a similar satisfaction for man's most basic drive and instinct, the desire to be coalesced with himself, others, and the world.

9

Death and Unification

AND FINALLY we come to death and the unification experience. Participants in dangerous sports, as we have seen, say that they participate in life-risking games for "kicks" or thrills. When queried further, they will indicate that they live most fully and intensely when they are racing, sky-diving, or climbing mountains. In other words, the risking of life adds to the buildup of the tension and the depth of the unification experience until it is finally resolved in orgasmic climax. The analogy to sexual experience is very close. Let us just look at mountain climbing, for instance. As someone first thinks of sex before indulging in sexual activity, so one thinks of climbing a mountain before making the actual attempt. The preparation depends on the degree of difficulty involved in the actual assault on the mountain. So the actual effort is preceded by a period of thinking, planning, and physical preparation.

An important point in all unification experiences is that once one begins to ruminate about a past activity associated with a unifying experience, or to anticipate such an experience, the process of unification commences. This fact is, of course, most visible in connection with sex which is the quintessential example. However, as we have seen, once one begins to think about the activity one unconsciously associates with unification satisfaction, the process tends to accelerate as other competing thoughts are repelled and as the mind prefers to dwell on the titillating ideas that are creating both a psychic and somatic tension preliminary to the orgasm of unification. But let us get back to the mountain.

Once the preparations are over and the actual climb begins, the mountaineer thinks fewer and fewer random thoughts. He then thinks primarily about the actual climbing, particularly if there is danger involved. His concern is just the next step and the next handhold. A mountaineer does of course think other thoughts and admire the landscape, at least when at rest or at the summit. As in sexual activity, his mind and body coalesce as both interact in perfect symbiosis. Mind and body become one. In mountain climbing, one becomes unified with oneself and nature in the form of the mountain, and with oneself and with others if one is climbing with companions. In climbing, the primary unity is established with oneself and the mountain before one merges with all. In heterosexual sexuality the primary unity is with a member of the opposite sex, in homosexuality it is with a member of the same sex, and in autoerotism, or unisexuality, it is with oneself.

The natural progression of our thought leads us from the

dangerous sports we have been discussing to suicide and death. Are not certain sports a prolonged form of suicide? Is this not particularly true of the drivers of Formula 1 cars on the Grand Prix circuit? Jimmy Clark, the winner of more Grand Prix races than any other driver in history, crashed and was killed at the age of thirty-three. Most drivers are killed sooner or later, and the "lucky" ones are those, like Stirling Moss, who survive with mangled bodies to show for their experience. Car racing of this sort is nothing but a long, drawn-out game of Russian roulette. Perhaps no other activity in all of sport creates so many and such prolonged states of unification. These men are always living on the narrow blade edge of life and death and are always under the greatest tension. Their lives are at risk at every moment. A small oil slick, a defective two-dollar part, a sudden shower, a miscalculation by another driver, or by themselves, can mean instant death. They are forced to concentrate until they are one with the machine, and at speeds exceeding two hundred miles an hour. They literally do not have time to think in the event of any trouble. Like the Zen swordsman, painter, or tea master, they must be one with what they are doing, and there can be no room for the discursive intellect, "I" consciousness, or egoistical affirmation.

These men are not self-destructive or imbued with a death wish as commonly thought by superficial psychoanalysts. Quite the contrary, they are very much in love with life and the greatest experience that life has to offer. They have savored the unification experience in a particularly intense form and seek to repeat it as frequently as possible. It should also be remarked that these men are not limited by age, physical condition, or economic circumstances to a narrow range of unification-producing experiences. They are generally young, attractive, have their pick of lovely women, and are constantly being feted and entertained. They are able to enjoy most of the activities of life that produce unification experiences, many of which are closed to others because of lack of opportunity or personal capacity.

The prototype of such a man was Don Alfonso Cabeza de Vaca y Leighton, seventeenth Marquis de Portago, who died in 1957 while racing his Grand Prix car in the Mille Miglia, in an accident that killed eleven persons and cut him in two at the age of twenty-eight.* Portago would have been unbelievable if encountered in fiction. He was larger than life-size, wealthy, married to a beauty, handsome, over six feet tall, and attractive to many men and women. In his short life he had many mistresses, and at his death he was involved in a much publicized romance with the motion picture actress Linda Christian. Portago was totally addicted to the activities that produce the most intense unification experiences—particularly love—and the sports where his life was constantly at risk.

At the age of seventeen he flew a borrowed aircraft under a bridge to win a $500 bet. He had been the leading

* Robert Daley, *Cars at Speed*, New York, Collier Books Edition, 1962. This is an excellent account of the sport of Grand Prix racing and the men who drive the Formula 1 cars. For the story of Portago's end, see Chapter I, "End of the Open Road," pp. 26–33.

amateur steeplechase jockey in the world, and in less than three full seasons on the Grand Prix circuit he had come to be recognized by his fellow drivers as the most daring of them all. In the dangerous sport of bobsledding, he narrowly missed winning an Olympic medal for Spain by only 17/100 of a second. This performance came after only a few practice runs in Switzerland, following which he bought a couple of sleds at a thousand dollars apiece, recruited a team among cousins from Madrid, and entered the Olympics.

Before his fatal accident, he had many narrow encounters with death. He was catapulted out of his bobsled on one of his initial runs when he lost control at sixty miles an hour. In his short driving career he walked away from some horrendous accidents. Like all sportsmen who risk their lives regularly, he found it difficult to explain his mania and compulsive obsession to put his life at stake at every opportunity. When pressed, he admitted that when his physical existence hung in the balance, all of his senses were sharpened and he felt most alive.

This is as close as most men who risk their lives week after week come to explaining why they do what they do. To those who knew Portago nothing could be more ridiculous than the "profound" psychoanalytic insight that he was in love with death. If anyone ever loved life it was the seventeenth Marquis de Portago who himself wrote of racing drivers: "Perhaps we appreciate life more, because we live closer to death." Robert Daley sums up the feelings he and others had about Portago: "He seemed to me the most alive man I had ever known. He was sensitive, restless, curiously gentle, and it is impossible to describe that impression of straining vitality which he communicated, nor to do justice to the overwhelming disbelief his friends felt when news of his death arrived."

Like most of us, Portago was a victim of the sleight-of-hand artist's deceptive trickery and focused on the activity rather than the experience. We, like him, tend to identify the experience with the sport or activity that produces it, and feel that we must indulge in that activity in order to re-create the experience. In actuality, it is something we can experience at any moment, in the most mundane aspect of life, and even at this very instant. All that is necessary is to let go of the thought process and the self; danger and death are not necessary to achieve the unification experience.

Death is the ultimate unification experience. As part of his eternal cycle and ceaseless becoming, man in death merges with himself, others, and all. Unification and death are the identical experience: one's true self is not something enclosed by our skin-encapsulated body, but is the entire universe. It is a moment of total silence; thought has ceased, and man ceases to identify with the ego, with its affirmations that are the self, with the discursive intellect, and with the thought process that has created them.

When we die or are unified, can we doubt that the false or pseudo self that we "fight to the death" to protect, perishes too? Can we doubt that the identification with the physical body also comes to an end? Can we doubt that all the doubts and fears of death and life cease to plague us? And can we doubt that the thought process itself terminates? It is the ultimate and final experience of unity, in which the body itself disintegrates and returns to the earth.

Some people seriously attempt suicide many times before they finally succeed, and some who try repeatedly never accomplish the act. Some forms of suicide are protracted: Russian roulette is one such variation. Jumping from high places is also an effort to prolong the process of suicide. Swimming out to sea beyond the point of no return is another example, and sleeping pills is still another. In fact, it may be suggested that most suicides take a longer time to accomplish than they need to. What the suicide is doing is prolonging and stretching the unification state as long as possible before he experiences his final, ultimate, and eternal orgasmic experience. Doomed convicts seem to be somewhat aware of death as the ultimate unification experience and have spoken of their coming execution as "the big ride," "the big slide," and "the last thrill."

One further comment may be made on the symbolic significance of certain suicidal acts, such as, jumping from high places, intentional drowning, and the taking of sleeping pills, which are all fairly commonplace ways of doing oneself in. Not only do all of these variants represent an obvious end of thinking and the thought process, but they also represent a physical merging with others, the world, and all, albeit in the case of jumping off buildings, out of windows, or from bridges, the merging is rather violent and forceful.

While the symbolism in the case of jumping or swimming is obvious, it is none the less apposite. The suicide in the commission of the act is rushing to merge physically with the earth or water, and frequently goes to his death with his arms held wide as though to embrace the source of his birth, to which he seeks to return. Water and earth, of course, represent not only man but the source of all we regard as life.

There is an analogy here to the search for the perfect sexual orgasm. Since time immemorial, or for as long as the recorded history of sexuality, man has attempted to perfect, prolong, and/or multiply the orgasm for himself and his partner. Timothy Leary, the high priest of LSD, has said in an interview in *Playboy* that multiple orgasm is the hidden secret of LSD and that it is possible to have several hundred orgasms in an hour under its influence. Supposedly, the secret of the late Aly Khan and other famous lovers was their ability to practice an oriental technique by which the male can engage in intercourse for a very long time without ejaculation, thus insuring maximum satisfaction to his female partner, who may enjoy many and repeated orgasms. The search by people of wealth for the perfect lover is well known, as in the case of Catherine of Russia, or among members of the so-called jet set, much of whose activity is a thinly veiled pretense concealing their overriding interest in self-satisfaction through sexual affairs.

One further point may be adduced in support of the general theory of unification. Does not "growing old" represent to most the loss of repetitive enjoyment of the activities most productive of unification experiences, such as, sexual relations, eating, drinking, dancing, and sports? Advancing age is feared because it means that man will be able to enjoy less and less those experiences that have given him his greatest pleasures. As these avenues of satisfaction are closed off to him, death becomes less fearsome and more and more friendly.

Without going deeply into the relationship of sleep to unification, sleep, even though we may dream frequently and violently, at least represents a cessation of totally conscious thought and a merging into a world that is less egotistically affirmed and more universal. Sleeping pills then represent a physically painless and relatively long, drawn-out merging with oneself, others, and the world. As we know from the personal experience we have all had, before we fall asleep our thoughts become fewer and fewer until they finally cease altogether. Just before losing consciousness we could not think even if we wanted to. So falling asleep is also a unification process that involves the gradual reduction of thought until there is no thought, and finally, unification ensues.

Death does not represent destruction, evil, meaningless oblivion, or the dark forces of man. It is the quintessence of what man has always desired most and what has been the chief motivational factor in his life, the search for, and repetition of, the spontaneous unification experiences he has encountered sporadically and at random during the course of his life and existence. It is the final, ultimate, and eternal experience of unity.

10

Conclusion

THE FEAR OF death is really a conglomerate composed of the fears of time, decay, the unknown, irreversibility, the loss of pleasurable sensations, the loss of thought, and the loss of self. We have seen, and personal observation must confirm, that much of what we call life is really pain and suffering. It is self-evident that we would gladly relinquish that part of our life which we call suffering. It is also apparent that much of life falls into that neutral gray area which we call vegetative existing, where we are not conscious of anything much happening. In this state we are not conscious of either physical or psychological pain or pleasure.

We have seen that we have taken a measurement, which we call clock time, and permitted it to tyrannize over and control our lives. This mind-created convention, instead of being a convenience, has become a dictator that imposes fearful pressure and tension upon us insofar as we believe that, like sand, it is constantly slipping through our fingers, in spite of our frantic efforts to contain the grains by keeping our fingers tightly squeezed together. Once we see time for the impostor that it is, and see how we have confused the measuring unit with the phenomenon which we are measuring, much if not all of our fear of time should be eliminated. While we are forced to live with conventional time insofar as it has imposed itself upon man, by the awareness of its essence we should at least be able to keep it in its place and not permit it to rule our lives.

We fear the unknown, decay, irreversibility, and transiency. Obviously, if the unknown becomes known, we no longer have any reason to fear it, and as we have seen, the condition of death is not as unknown to us as we think it is. But do we not live with the unknown all the time? Do we know what is going to happen the next moment which, even as we think of it, becomes *now* and the past? Do we know what lurks around the next corner, be it a literal or a figurative one? Do we know whom we will meet next, and what they will say? In this sense we are always living with the unknown. Why then should we be fearful of it?

We also fear that we will not persist in the same form we are now. We must accept the fact that there are many things we do not know and in all likelihood will not know. But we do know that there are periods in our life, of which we are presently amnesic, when we existed in the physical form with which we are most familiar. And is not life in all forms characterized by the cycle of birth, death, and rebirth and regeneration? Why should we fear what happens to us after death if we do not fear the state before our birth? Is this not relevant? And is not the question *Who were we before our birth?* important? What we really fear most, do we not? is the loss of our pleasurable sensations, our thoughts, our thinking ability, and our self.

When one relinquishes his self, he lets go of his thoughts, self-consciousness, and the thought process, and he achieves unification. The unification experience is identical with the loss of the self. The loss of this pseudo self is precisely what is achieved in the moment of unification. Just as man reaches out for this experience, so he desires to be rid of the false self, which is an unconscious encumbrance in that it is insatiable and must be constantly nurtured; the more it is fed, the greater is its hunger. This self, as we have seen, is made up of shifting chimeras with no more reality than any other single, random, or stray thought. It is this self that alienates man from himself, others, and the world in which he dwells. This is the self that obscures his real nature, and is the basic source of his existential anxiety, which represents fear of the future, regret over the past, and concern over the ever-elusive present. It is this anxiety which man calls unhappiness. This self, along with its creator, the thought process, is what prevents man from living and being truly alive; it identifies with the concept of living rather than with his vegetative existence, which he shares not only with animals and plants but with so-called inert matter.

Nor is this viewpoint anti-intellectual. Many of man's unification experiences can come through thought or mental activity. Intellectual insights and investigations have resulted in unification experiences, just as man's more physical activities have. *Raja* yoga, the way of the intellect, is recognized as just as traditional and valid a path to *nirvana* as the physical *hatha* yoga techniques. We do not inveigh against the employment of the intellect, but rather against its chronic misuse, when it becomes, like time, a Golem or Frankenstein monster that tyrannizes its own creator. When this happens, man is even further alienated not only from himself but from his own mind as well.

Much of man's behavior is motivated by his desire for repetitive experiences of unification; between his fear of death and his desire for the unifying experience, a large part of his total culture can be explained. This culture includes his art, literature, books, motion pictures, drama, dance, music, poetry, song, and comedy in addition to the sports and other activities we have discussed. Do not many of these forms give the reader, viewer, or watcher a vicarious unification experience? The experience may be vicarious insofar as one obtains it as an auditor, reader, or spectator, but it is just as real as one attained more directly. Are not literary and artistic works judged, albeit unconsciously, in large measure by the degree to which they can produce or evoke an experience of unity in man? Is not this, perhaps, the secret hallmark and universal standard we use to evaluate great works of art and great men?

Have we not seen that man's greatest happiness comes when he lets go of not only thought but the very process of thinking itself? Man is also fearful of letting go of the false or pseudo self that he has so carefully nurtured since his birth. This is a self composed of nothing but thoughts, but thoughts with a difference, the difference being that he has given these thoughts greater importance and significance by more constant reiteration than his other thoughts.

Are we not basically afraid of death because we simply do not know what it is, and because no reliable report has ever come back from the dead? But suppose we do know what death is. Would not this alleviate most of the terror associated with our finitude?

We do know what death is. Does not everything we know about the condition of death accord and conform with what we know about the experience of unification? And is not this experience the one man most avidly seeks during his lifetime? Should he not welcome it when it comes? Is it not something that he is really quite familiar with, having tasted it many times during his lifetime? Why should he fear what is apparently a permanent condition and state of unification? The point of this book is that what we think we dread above all else is really what we most desire. Death, which has frightened man since his emergence as a thinking creature, is his ultimate and eternal unification experience. Death comes to all, not as a scourge or punishment, but as the culmination and fulfillment of life.